The Open University

Business School

Block 1
Social Marketing

Prepared for the B324 Team
by Anne Smith

This publication forms part of an Open University module B324. Details of this and other Open University modules can be obtained from the Student Registration and Enquiry Service, The Open University, PO Box 197, Milton Keynes MK7 6BJ, United Kingdom: tel. +44 (0)870 333 4340, email general-enquiries@open.ac.uk

Alternatively, you may visit the Open University website at www.open.ac.uk where you can learn more about the wide range of modules and packs offered at all levels by The Open University.

To purchase a selection of Open University module materials visit www.ouw.co.uk, or contact Open University Worldwide, Michael Young Building, Walton Hall, Milton Keynes MK7 6AA, United Kingdom for a brochure (tel. +44 (0)1908 858793; fax +44 (0)1908 858787; email ouwenq@open.ac.uk).

The Open University, Walton Hall, Milton Keynes, MK7 6AA

First published 2008. Second edition 2011.

Edited and designed by The Open University.

Printed in the United Kingdom by Cambrian Printers, Aberystwyth

The paper used in this publication is procured from forests independently certified to the level of Forest Stewardship Council (FSC) principles and criteria. Chain of custody certification allows the tracing of this paper back to specific forest-management units (see www.fsc.org).

FSC
Mixed Sources
Product group from well-managed forests and other controlled sources
Cert no. TT-COC-2200
www.fsc.org
© 1996 Forest Stewardship Council

ISBN 978 1 8487 3590 3

2.1

Contents

1 Introduction

Never before have social issues been more at the centre of public and private debate than at present. From concerns about sustainability and the future of the planet to the introduction of smoking bans; from actions to combat 'binge drinking' and childhood obesity to programmes designed to prevent the spread of AIDS in developing countries, there is a growing recognition that social marketing has a role to play in achieving a wide range of social goals. In the UK for example the National Social Marketing Centre (NSMC) has been established by the Department of Health and the National Consumer Council. You may wish to visit the NSMC website, which illustrates the interest in social marketing and health issues. A link is provided on the B324 website.

This block examines the nature of social marketing and how the adoption of marketing concepts, frameworks and techniques developed for commercial marketers can be applied to the solution of social problems. Primarily, social marketing aims to effect behavioural change in the pursuit of social goals and objectives, as opposed to financial or other objectives. There is a growing body of research and development in the area. The Institute for Social Marketing, a collaboration between the Open University and the University of Stirling, has a history of social marketing research spanning 30 years. Many of the examples and case studies are derived from this work and are included in a recent textbook by Gerard Hastings (2007), 'Social marketing: why should the Devil have all the best tunes?'. This is the core text for this block and the sections in this 'wraparound' are designed to guide you through the book, and the many activities within it, while adding some additional material. Two other readings are included in the resource pack for Block 1. The first, 'Broadening the concept of marketing' by Kotler and Levy (1969) is generally considered to be the seminal article in this subject area. As well as presenting the key message, that marketing can be applied to social and other not-for-profit issues, this paper serves as a reminder of the core elements of marketing planning, illustrated in nine key points. The second paper by Kotler and Zaltman (1971) is entitled 'Social marketing: an approach to planned social change'. This presents a framework for the development of social marketing planning and an important reminder that social marketing should not be confused with social advertising. Both of these readings are included in the appendices at the end of this wraparound.

Reading

Reading

1.1 Aims and objectives

The aims of this block are to:

- explore how marketing concepts and techniques can be applied to the marketing of social issues as opposed to the more traditional area of commercial marketing
- examine how social marketing approaches can change behaviour in order to achieve socially desirable goals

- illustrate, through case study examples, the application of concepts and techniques to 'real world' social marketing problems.

On completing this unit you should be able to:

- describe and explain the meaning and nature of social marketing
- analyse social marketing problems and suggest ways of solving these
- prepare a social marketing plan for a range of organisations
- apply marketing tools and techniques, e.g. market segmentation and targeting; marketing mix frameworks; relationship marketing approaches, to a range of social issues and organisational contexts
- assess the role of service organisations in the development and delivery of social marketing programmes
- assess the role of social advertising and other communications in achieving behavioural change
- explain how social marketing techniques and concepts can achieve behavioural change
- develop a social marketing research plan as a basis for decision making
- recognise the role of ethics in developing and implementing social marketing programmes and plans
- Develop a plan for evaluating social marketing programmes/activites.

1.2 Module structure

The module is structured into ten main sections:

- Section 1 is this introduction.
- Section 2 introduces the key elements of social marketing and asks why this approach is relevant and necessary in today's environment.
- Section 3 focuses on the nature of behaviour. Since social marketing programmes aim to achieve behavioural change, an understanding of consumer/human behavioural models is essential for developing appropriate actions and interventions.
- Section 4 is the largest element of the module as it focuses on the development of the social marketing plan. To guide you through this section, Figure 4.1 has been borrowed from the core text. This illustrates the sub-sections of the marketing planning process, i.e. situation analysis; stakeholder analysis; market segmentation and targeting; objective setting and marketing mix development. The marketing mix section, which examines concepts such as 'price' and 'place' within a social marketing context, also focuses on the ways in which services play an important part in the delivery of many programmes. Finally, within this section the important elements of communication and branding are examined.
- Section 5 adds an important dimension to the discussion by considering audiences (or target markets) other than the final consumer for social marketers to address. A focus on these individuals/groups/organisations is described by Hastings as moving upstream and includes government policy makers and collaborators such as those service organisations described in the previous section.

- Section 6 develops the previous discussion by focusing on a relationship marketing approach to social marketing. This is as relevant to the final consumer as to those stakeholders described in Section 5 and derives from the growing acknowledgement in both marketing theory and practice that the transactions approach of the marketing mix fails to recognise the factors that influence behaviour.

- Section 7 examines the important contribution that marketing research makes to understanding consumers and developing effective programmes for behavioural change.

- Section 8 considers the ethical issues that should concern social marketers as they develop and deliver their programmes to achieve social goals.

- Section 9 focuses on the issues involved in evaluating social marketing programmes.

- Finally, Section 10 presents a brief summary and conclusion.

After you have completed the various sections and associated readings, you may like to answer the self-assessment questions (SAQs) which follow. The answers can be found after the references.

Table 1.1 indicates the block sections and sub-sections, the relevant reading for each of these and the main case studies from the core text, which are included as activities in the various sections.

Table 1.1 Social marketing – structure, readings and cases

Section	Textbook reference*	Cases	Additional reading
1 Introduction			
2 Understanding the nature of social marketing	Chapter 1		Kotler and Levy (1969) 'Broadening the Concept of Marketing', *Journal of Marketing*, vol. 33, no. 1, pp. 10–15
3 Understanding consumer behaviour	Chapter 2		
4 Social marketing planning			
4.1 Situation analysis	Chapter 3	Case Study 11: 'The challenges of using social marketing in India: The case of HIV/AIDS prevention'	
4.2 Stakeholder analysis	Chapter 8		
4.3 Market segmentation and targeting	Chapter 4		
4.4 Social marketing objectives		Case Study 3: 'A social advertising strategy to reduce speeding'	

4.5 The marketing mix and the service element in social marketing		Case 10: 'Physicians taking action against smoking'	
4.6 The role of communications and branding in social marketing programmes	Chapter 5	Case Study 15: 'Be well, know your BGL. Diabetes: Australia's diabetes awareness campaign'	Kotler, P. and Zaltman, G. (1971) 'Social marketing: an approach to planned social change', *Journal of Marketing*, vol. 35, no. 3, pp. 3–12
5 The social marketing network, moving upstream	Chapter 6		
6 Relationship marketing	Chapter 7	Case Study 14: 'Using the internet to reach upstream and downstream in social marketing programmes'	
7 The role of research in social marketing	Chapter 9	Case Study 17: 'Community-based social marketing to promote positive mental health', The Act–Belong–Commit campaign in rural Western Australia	
8 The role of ethics in social marketing	Chapter 10		
9 Evaluating social marketing programmes			
10 Conclusion			

*Textbook: Hastings, G. (2007) *Social Marketing: why should the Devil have all the best tunes?* Elsevier/Butterworth Heinemann.

2 Understanding the nature of social marketing

Before we focus on 'social marketing' we should clarify the nature of 'marketing' as both an academic discipline and a management practice.

Kotler and Armstrong (2008, p. 5) define marketing as:

> Marketing is a social and managerial process by which individuals and organisations obtain what they need and want through creating and exchanging value with others.

Two further definitions are:

> Marketing is the management process responsible for identifying, anticipating and satisfying customer requirements profitably.
>
> (Source: Chartered Institute of Marketing, 2007, www.cim.co.uk)

And:

> Marketing is an organizational function and a set of processes for creating, communicating and delivering value to customers and for managing customer relationships in ways that benefit the organization and its stakeholders.
>
> (Source: American Marketing Association, 2004, p. 3)

A number of key issues are highlighted by these definitions:

- *Exchange* – most explicitly noted in Kotler's and Armstrong's definition is the core element of exchange. In commercial marketing the nature of the exchange is usually clear, i.e. a product or service for money. Although a closer analysis often reveals that even here things are not so simple, for example, the price can be considered to include time spent in obtaining the product.
- *Customer satisfaction* – The pivotal construct in marketing is that of customer satisfaction. Commercial marketers aim to satisfy customers to a greater extent than the competition. Satisfaction is considered to lead to behaviour such as positive word of mouth, repeat purchase and ultimately, profitability. In the definitions, this is illustrated by reference to customer needs, wants and the satisfaction of requirements.
- *Goals and objectives* – Marketing exchange takes place so as to achieve the goals of the buyer and the seller. For commercial marketers these goals may be profit, market share etc., for the individual the goals may be the self-esteem achieved by buying an expensive car. A major difference between commercial and social marketing lies in the difference in the nature of the goals and objectives. Here the goals are society's goals.
- *Process* – All definitions emphasise the processes which the marketer must undertake. Customer needs and requirements must be identified

9

through a process of market research, supplied through the development of a product, at the right price, through appropriate channels and using effective promotion.

- *Value* – Two of the definitions emphasise the need for value. A key question for social marketers is the need to establish the value of the 'product' on offer – exactly what is being offered in terms of value to people who adopt new behaviours such as recycling or stopping smoking?

2.1 So how should social marketing be defined?

Read Chapter 1 in the core text.

Make a note of the key characteristics of social marketing as defined by the National Social Marketing Centre (NSMC) (illustrated in Box 1.1), and Lazer and Kelley's (1973) definition of social marketing. You will find further definitions in Box 3.1 in Chapter 3.

The definition offered by Kotler et al. (2002, p. 5) is also a useful one:

> The use of marketing principles and techniques to influence a target audience to voluntarily accept, reject, modify or abandon a behaviour for the benefit of individuals, groups or society as a whole.

Social marketing relies on voluntary compliance rather than legal, economic or coercive forms of influence.

Kotler et al. (2002) argue that social marketing is often used to influence an audience to change their behaviour for the sake of:

- improving health – health issues
- preventing injuries – safety issues
- protecting the environment – environmental issues
- contributing to the community – community-building issues.

Activity 2.1

Think for a moment about familiar examples of social marketing.

Comment

One of the most obvious examples is that of the anti-smoking campaigns. Here it is important to note Hastings' point that social advertising and social marketing are not the same thing. From the public's perception this is often the 'face' of social marketing but for the marketer many other issues must be taken into account as illustrated by the NSMC's outline. Other current examples relate to the many initiatives to reduce energy consumption; encourage recycling; reduce binge drinking, and many more.

Activity 2.2

Now listen to the podcast – What is Social Marketing? by Gerard Hastings and Michaela Firth (UK National Health Service)

In this podcast Michaela asks Gerard to explain both what social marketing is, and to explain its benefits to her as a health service practitioner. Gerard explains some of the key principles of social marketing including: the need to understand customers by conducting a range of market research activities (large scale – quantitative and small scale – qualitative); the need to build trust with customers and emphasise customer loyalty as a goal; the need to take a strategic planning perspective in showing how social marketing fits into the wider activities and plans of the health service trust. He emphasises that marketing and communication are not the same thing. He also emphasises that in some cases there is a need to segment and target the market involving differentiation of the product offering but at other times a global standardised perspective can be adopted.

Michaela also asks the important question of how to get health professionals to understand and accept social marketing as an approach, including suggestions as to how she can convince her boss to allocate funding to social marketing activities.

2.2 Reasons for social marketing

Your readings and thoughts should already have suggested reasons why social marketing can be an effective approach to dealing with social problems and issues. We will now consider some of these as well as arguments against the use of marketing within this context.

- *The power of marketing* – The power of marketing principles and techniques in the hands of the commercial sector cannot be denied and many examples were provided in Chapter 1 of the core text. Most of us, including very young children, recognise logos and brand names, even for products that we never buy. These symbols occupy our minds and form part of our sociocultural context. Many of us will spend our hard-earned money by paying well above the functional utility price of a product in order to acquire a specific brand name that means something to us. Consider for example, how branding plays a part in our choice of baked beans, soap powder, clothing, watches and cars. Communication through the various media is clearly very powerful, consequently it would seem negligent, to say the least, not to adapt this power to society's good. As Gerard Hastings' book title says – 'Why should the Devil have all the best tunes?'

- *Track record/evidence* – There are many examples of social marketing applications which have been successful in achieving positive behavioural change. We will look at some of these throughout the block.

- *Not an option* – As Kotler and Levy argue in their article (see below), 'the choice … is not whether to market or not to market … The choice is whether to do it well or poorly' (p. 15).

2.3 Reasons against social marketing

- *Cost* – Social marketing programmes can cost considerable amounts of money. Criticisms of these expenditures are heightened as they are often financed by public money in times of resource constraints and therefore have a high opportunity cost. A related issue is that of the problems involved in assessing the success of these programmes. The long-term nature of behavioural change and the difficulties in establishing cause–effect relationships add to the fuel for the critics.

- *Misconceptions and negative attitudes about marketing* – As most introductory marketing textbooks relate, marketing is often equated with selling and persuading people to buy things that they do not really want. Interestingly, when people are asked if they have been persuaded they usually say no. Today's adoption of marketing principles and techniques (for example, market segmentation, market research, branding) by the banking sector is now evident. It was not too long ago, however, that bank managers were describing such activity as 'nauseating', 'odious and irrelevant' and 'an overrated pastime' (Turnbull and Wootton, 1980, p. 482). Many professional services such as accountants and solicitors still equate marketing with advertising (Barr and McNeilly, 2003). Public sector organisations, such as hospital trusts, have also been slow to adopt (Meidan et al., 2000). Lack of awareness of the potential of marketing, misunderstanding and the observation of some of the more doubtful practices of the commercial sector are some of the reasons behind this. You may have noted in Chapter 1 that Hastings also includes the criticism of commercial marketing as an element of social marketing and this is highlighted in the Lazer and Kelley definition. A final reason for resistance to marketing may be due to the nature of the language. Strategic marketing, for example, adopts the terminology of Sun Zu's 'The Art of War' (Krause, 1995). Phrases such as 'flanking defence', 'encirclement' and 'full frontal attack' are probably not particularly attractive to the National Health Service (NHS) or Oxfam.

- *Parameters of marketing activity* – A final point emerges from marketing authors themselves. In response to Kotler and Levy's article 'Broadening the concept of marketing' (see below) Luck (1969) argued that the wider application of marketing away from the commercial sector dilutes the content and nature of marketing as a discipline. There are few proponents of this view, however, and the last four decades have seen many applications including, of course, the application of social marketing.

Activity 2.3

Reading

i   Read Kotler and Levy's article 'Broadening the concept of marketing' (1969). (See Appendix 1).

There are two reasons for reading this article:

First, it will serve as a reminder, for those of you who have studied marketing previously, of some of the key elements of marketing theory and practice. For those who have not studied marketing it will provide a grounding to underpin subsequent discussion.

Second, although not concerned solely with social marketing, this is considered to be a key paper in bringing the concepts and techniques of marketing to the much wider context of not-for-profit, social and cause marketing applications.

ii   Make a note of the nine concepts listed in the article. I will draw your attention to where these are discussed as we move through the sections. The first, 'generic product definition', is discussed below.

2.4 Generic product definition

Kotler and Levy (1969) emphasise the need to define products in terms of the customer needs being served. This idea was developed further in an article by Theodore Levitt in 1981. He argued that in addition to the basic product that people buy there are the augmented elements of service, delivery, financing etc., which add value to a tangible product. Levitt's approach is a useful one for thinking about the differences between tangible goods and services. The basic/tangible product is augmented by the service elements, for example; the tangible product of a washing machine is augmented by delivery, installation and after sales service. However, for a service such as a flight, it is the tangible elements which augment the intangible service offering, such as the appearance of the aircraft cabin and crew and in flight food and drink. For both, the core benefit can be identified; i.e. clean clothes and transport.

So what is the social marketing product?

This is probably one of the most difficult questions to answer, particularly since it may vary from one consumer to another. Many social marketing programmes are based around promoting health. Consumers are buying better health and longevity from giving up smoking for example. However for some market segments, e.g. younger people, this is not considered an important issue. So what are they buying? One core benefit which has been communicated in previous campaigns has been 'attractiveness to potential partners'. This has emphasised the unpleasant smell of cigarette smoke. Another core benefit has been 'social acceptability'. This has been emphasised through drawing attention to the anti-social aspects such as the effects of passive smoking.

As you look at the various case studies in the core text, ask yourself what the nature of the core benefit is and note how this is often augmented through tangible elements such as promotional materials.

In the next section we look at another of Kotler and Levy's key concepts 'customer behaviour analysis' and again focus on the nature of the exchange in social marketing.

3 Understanding consumer behaviour

Andreasen (1995) states that for the social marketer 'consumer behaviour is the bottom line' (p. 14). In order to understand how to develop programmes that will bring about behavioural change we need to understand something about the nature of behaviour. The consumer behaviour literature typically borrows from the fields of sociology, psychology and social anthropology amongst others. There is a vast, and growing, body of knowledge on the subject and a few of the main elements will be discussed in this section, which highlights some of the points presented in Chapter 2 of the core text.

Key elements of consumer behaviour include:

(a) analysis of the factors which influence behaviour

(b) the role of motivation and attitudes

(c) consumer behaviour models.

 Read Chapter 2 and try Exercises 2.1 and 2.4.

Note that the issue of marketing as exchange was discussed in Section 2 of this wraparound. You might like to revisit this while reading Chapter 2 of the core text.

3.1 The factors which influence consumer behaviour

A large number of factors influence our behaviour. Kotler and Armstrong (2008) classify these as:

- *psychological* (motivation, perception, learning, beliefs and attitudes)
- *personal* (age and life-cycle stage, occupation, economic circumstances, lifestyle, personality and self concept)
- *social* (reference groups, family, roles and status)
- *cultural* (culture, sub-culture, social class system).

On the next page you will see Figure 3.1 which appears in Chapter 2 of the core text. This adapts the above factors to a health behaviour context, providing a model which also explicitly emphasises, together with cultural factors, other features such as the economic environment as an element of the wider social context.

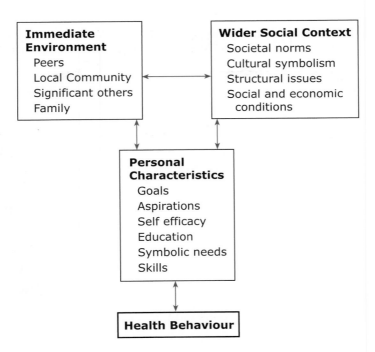

Figure 3.1 The wider determinants of health behaviour

(Source: Hastings, 2007)

As you can see, the immediate environment approximates to Kotler's social factors. Many studies of both commercial and social marketing emphasise the influence of family, friends and others on our decisions. Peer group pressure is an important influence and may be negative or positive.

The diagram illustrates an approach known as social-cognitive theory which is based on the proposition that our behaviour is determined by both personal and environmental factors.

3.2 The importance of understanding motivation and attitudes

Personal characteristics in Figure 3.1 combine both psychological and personal factors. Two important factors which drive behaviour are motivation and attitudes.

The importance of understanding motivation

MacFadyen et al. (1998) (see Figure 3.1) emphasise the role of goals, aspirations and symbolic needs. Many of you will be familiar with theories of motivation and how they explain why we engage in a particular behaviour in order to achieve our goals and satisfy our needs. There are many theories of motivation. You may have come across these in other studies of marketing, human resource management or elsewhere. Motivation theories seek to explain why we do the things we do either by examining how a behaviour satisfies our 'needs' or the processes we go through as we decide how to achieve our goals. One of the best known motivation theories is Maslow's (1943) theory of human motivation or hierarchy of needs. The five original needs comprised those listed and illustrated in the typical hierarchical approach in Figure 3.2.

1 *Physiological needs*: These are the basic needs of the organism such as food, water, oxygen and sleep. They also include the somewhat less basic needs such as sex or activity.

2 *Safety needs*: Here Maslow is talking about the need for a generally ordered existence in a stable environment which is relatively free of threats to the safety of a person's existence.

3 *Social (love) needs*: These are the need for affectionate relations with other individuals and the need for one to have a recognised place as a group member – the need to be accepted by one's peers.

4 *Esteem needs*: The need of a stable, firmly based self-evaluation. The need for self-respect, self-esteem, and for the esteem of others.

5 *Self-actualisation needs*: The need for self-fulfilment. The need to achieve one's full capacity.

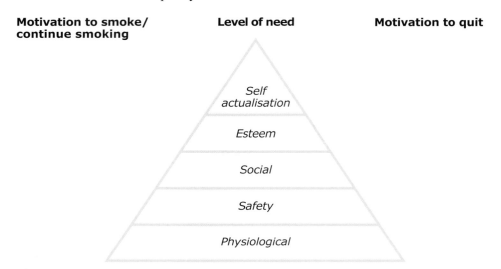

Figure 3.2a Maslow's Hierarchy of Needs: Motivations to smoke and to quit

Activity 3.1

By reference to Maslow's hierarchy in Figure 3.2a, illustrate for each level of need why you think that young people (teenagers) are motivated to smoke and why they might be motivated to quit.

Comment

Figure 3.2b (overleaf) has been completed with some of the reasons to smoke, and to stop smoking, added. In addition, money could be a motivator at various levels, e.g. spending money on family or friends (social needs) or to avoid debt (safety needs) or to achieve self-esteem through purchase of an expensive mobile phone.

Motivation to smoke/ continue smoking	Level of need	Motivation to quit
Part of one's self concept /personality/image	Self actualisation	Rising above the pressure of advertisers and addiction
Esteem of one's smoking peers for not succumbing to parental and other social pressures to quit	Esteem	Self esteem and the esteem of others for success in beating a powerful addiction
Peer pressure	Social	Impact of passive smoking
Being one of a group		Being an outcast
As a response to stressful situations	Safety	Fear of severe illness
	Physiological	Improved health
Nicotine dependency		

Figure 3.2b Maslow's Hierarchy of Needs: Motivations to smoke and to quit

The importance of understanding attitudes

One of the most important phenomena for a social marketer to understand is that of 'attitudes'. Having said this, this is not a straightforward issue as there is much disagreement about the nature of attitudes, how they are formed and how they determine our behaviour. Attitude theory research is a key focus for consumer behaviour theorists and derives from the field of psychology.

There are many definitions of attitude, for example, 'the predisposition of the individual to evaluate some symbol or object or aspect of his world in a favourable manner' (Katz, 1970).

There are also differences of opinion as to what comprises an attitude. The three main elements on which theorists focus are:

- Cognitive component (beliefs/knowledge).
- Affective component (feelings).
- Conative component (behavioural).

In other words we believe/know (cognitive component) something, for example, recycling is good for the environment. We also believe that looking after the environment is a good thing. This forms our positive feelings (affect) towards recycling behaviour. We are therefore more likely to intend to engage in recycling behaviour (conative factor) and ultimately to engage in the behaviour itself.

Differences of opinion relate to which of the three components are actually part of attitude:

- Some (e.g. Fishbein, 1970) view attitude as a relatively simple unidimensional construct referring to the amount of affect for or against a psychological object (in other words the feeling element only).
- Others (e.g. Bagozzi and Bunkrant, 1979) describe attitude as a two-dimensional construct including the cognitive and affective components.

- Others (e.g. Katz and Stotland, 1959) describe attitude as a complex multi-dimensional concept consisting of affective, cognitive and behavioural components.

In one sense the above distinction does not matter too much since all approaches recognise the three components. However, it is important when we come to measure attitudes to be clear as to what exactly is being measured. The most important issue for us at the moment is to be aware of the three components and how they combine to determine behaviour. Most of the research in this area is based on Fishbein and Ajzen's (1975) theory of reasoned action described in the model below.

The theories of reasoned action and planned behaviour

The extended Fishbein model, based on the theory of reasoned action includes the following components to explain behaviour.

(a) Attitude to the behaviour comprising:

(i) The strength of the expectancy (beliefs) that the act will be followed by a consequence.

(ii) The value of that consequence to the individual.

This is the basic expectancy value approach. Returning to our previous smoking cessation example, if we expect that stopping smoking will result in health, wealth and happiness – and this is important to us, then we will develop a positive affect towards the behaviour of stopping smoking. There is, however another dimension.

(b) Subjective norms (i.e. the sociocultural norms of other persons, groups or society) and the individuals' desire/motivation to conform to these norms. Consequently, peer group and other pressures may reduce or enhance our attitudes towards stopping smoking. Ajzen (1985) later included:

(c) Perceived control (i.e. situational or internal obstacles to performing the behaviour). This addition has resulted in a new model – 'the theory of planned behaviour'. Consequently, the power of addiction may impact on our attitudes and prevent us from trying to stop smoking.

A key question, for both commercial and social marketers is – *'Why do actual behaviour and reported intentions often differ?'*

As discussed earlier, the purpose of social marketing is to effect behaviour change. Attitude models often record behavioural intentions rather than actual behaviour. One of the purposes of research is to assess how people will behave in the future, for example in response to new stimuli such as additional resources – help lines, clinics etc. One of the problems, however, is that reported behavioural intentions often don't match up to actual behaviour.

Activity 3.2

List the reasons why you think that what people say they will do in answer to research questions is often very different to what they actually do.

Comment

There are many reasons. These may include:

- Reasons to do with the research process. For example; telling the researcher what they want to know out of politeness.
- Reasons to do with the individual's wish to show themselves to be rational or a 'good citizen'. They might, therefore, overstate intentions to reduce environmental emissions and understate intentions to use private transport.
- They may genuinely intend to engage in the behaviour but situational factors intervene – they may not have the time to travel by public transport or there may be a bus strike.

3.3 Consumer behaviour models

Many theorists have developed models of consumer behaviour. Some of these focus on the factors that influence behaviour (such as the model in Figure 3.1). Others emphasise the stages that consumers go through as they make their decisions to engage in a particular behaviour. Many adopt the 'belief–feeling–behavioural intention' behaviour model illustrated in Section 3.2.

The 'stages' approach has been adapted by social marketers in the stages of change model discussed in Chapter 2 of the core text. It is worth reiterating the point made by Hastings in Chapter 2: Theories and models help us to make sense of the world by distilling previous learning but can never explain it perfectly. All such theories and models have their limitations and these should be recognised.

4 Social marketing planning

A planning approach to marketing is considered to have several advantages, for example; it provides clarity of direction (which is a motivator), a yardstick for evaluation, and a framework for effective resource allocation. In our introductory paper Kotler and Levy (1969) referred to this as 'integrated marketing planning'. Figure 3.3 from the core text is reproduced below as Figure 4.1. This provides a framework for a social marketing plan and is the basis for the following sections. In Section 4.1 we focus on situation analysis; in Section 4.2 we examine the stakeholders; in Section 4.3, market segmentation and targeting; in Section 4.4, setting social marketing objectives; in Section 4.5, formulating the offer (the marketing and services mix) and finally in Section 4.6 we look at promotion, communications and branding in more detail.

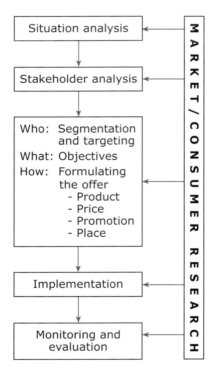

Figure 4.1 The social marketing plan

(Source: Hastings, 2007)

4.1 Situation analysis

A situation (or situational) analysis, as the name suggests, involves an appraisal of the current situation including both internal and external factors. Referring back to Kotler and Levy's nine elements in Activity 2.2 we are now addressing the 'marketing audit' which also requires an assessment of the organisation, its strengths, weaknesses and capabilities. The following discussion emphasises approaches to external analysis and also an appreciation of the nature and role of external and internal stakeholders.

There are many ways of classifying external factors, for example, you will probably have come across the PEST (political, economic, social (or sociocultural), technological) acronym for 'macro-environmental' factors or possibly the STEEPLE (Sociocultural, technological, economic, ethical, political, legal, environmental) approach. Here environmental factors refer to the 'green issues' and as this is likely to be a focus of social marketing planning you need to be clear whether you are describing the wider environmental factors or the term as it applies to the ecological environment. In addition to the macro-environmental factors there are a whole range of what are sometimes described as micro-environmental factors. These include suppliers, distributors, the public etc. These organisations/groups/individuals will comprise the stakeholders of the organisation and will be the focus of the next section.

One final group of stakeholders which operates within the micro-environment is the competition. As Hastings (2007) emphasises in Chapter 8, there is a need for careful analysis of exactly what competition means in the context of social marketing. It might, for example, include other organisations supplying the same product or those encouraging the competing behaviour. Before we go on to look at the nature of stakeholders try the following activity. You will find the case study in the core text.

Activity 4.1

Identify and classify the environmental factors which are relevant to Case Study 11: 'The challenges of using social marketing in India: the case of HIV/AIDS prevention'.

Do these factors pose opportunities or threats to the development and implementation of this social marketing programme?

Comment

The following problems or threats can be identified. These can be listed under the headings of political, economic and sociocultural.

Political

- Lack of state healthcare.
- Lack of sex education (e.g. in schools).
- Resources devoted to the problem.
- Government attitudes towards AIDS prevention.
- Expertise in the development and delivery of programmes.
- Non-governmental organisations (NGOs) lack of expertise and resources.
- Government policy on AIDS prevention.

Economic

- Population size.
- Geographical area.
- Low income levels.
- Price of healthcare.
- Distribution system for condoms.

Sociocultural

- Prevalence of heterosexual activity involving commercial sex workers.
- Lack of awareness/understanding of AIDS.
- Inhibitions about discussing sex.
- Negative attitudes to condoms.
- Low literacy rates.
- Prejudice towards people living with HIV/AIDS.
- Cultural diversity, e.g. number of languages and religions.
- Level of corruption.

There are however some opportunities or positive environmental trends which can be considered:

- A more general global understanding of HIV/AIDS.
- Advances in treatment.
- Improvements in communication technologies.
- Awareness and interest amongst organisations (e.g. NGOs).

NB. Environmental factors are interrelated. By phrasing a specific issue in a different way this can alter the classification. For example, is the last factor, level of corruption, a feature of the sociocultural or political environment? It could be either.

 Now read Chapter 3 of the core text.

4.2 Stakeholder analysis

Greenley and Foxall (1998) emphasise that the marketing literature typically focuses on only two stakeholder groups (consumers and competitors) arguing that this should be extended to include other key stakeholders. Freeman (1984) highlights the interdependence of organisations and their stakeholders, 'any group or individual who can affect or is affected by the achievement of the organisation's objectives' (p. 46). This definition emphasises the wide range of individuals, groups and organisations who/ which might have an interest in social marketing programmes.

Gerard Hastings makes a similar point in Chapter 6 which he describes as 'moving upstream'. Discussion of social marketing typically focuses on the individual or groups of individuals whose behaviour change is the aim of the programme or activity. Yet there are many organisations and individuals with which and with whom it is important for social marketers to engage, for example, government bodies and service providers who may also require information.

Figure 4.2 Stakeholder interest in health related social marketing programmes

(Source: Fischbacher, 2005)

A major concern of decision makers is the need to balance the often conflicting expectations and interests of stakeholders. Stakeholder analysis asks:

- Who are the stakeholders in a particular issue or activity?
- What are the expectations and objectives of the various stakeholder groups?
- What are their interests and how interested are they?

How dependent is the organisation on each group and how is this changing over time? In terms of:

- the degree of power (potential for disruption) that the group exercises
- possibility of replacing the relationship
- extent of uncertainty in the relationship.

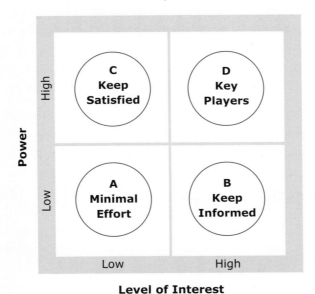

Figure 4.3 Stakeholder mapping: The Power/Interest matrix (Mendelow)

(Source: adapted from Johnson and Scholes, 1999)

Mendelow's matrix (see Figure 4.3) describes four types of stakeholder. It should be noted that the classifications are context specific and dynamic, for example, stakeholders in Group C may move into Group D if their interest in a particular project increases. Additionally, those in Group B may become empowered by access to key players, media attention etc.

Activity 4.2

Refer back to Case Study 11. If you were developing this social marketing campaign, which stakeholder groups would you have to take into consideration? Use Mendelow's matrix to classify the groups according to their interest and power.

Comment

There are many stakeholder groups involved. You may have made a number of assumptions in your analysis so make sure that these have been clearly stated.

- Central government – D. They have control over resources and ultimate responsibility for success. There may be lack of interest in some parts of government, or influences due to corruption etc...

- Non-government organisations (NGOs) – B. Low in resources but interested in the success of the programme. We do not, however, know about other sources of power such as the ability to influence or exert political pressure.

- Department for International Development – as NGOs above.

- Retailers/potential retailers of condoms – C. High power as they can control the supply of condoms but because of the various cultural influences they have little interest in the issue. However as the programme proceeds they may become key players.

- Consumer groups – A. The various consumer groups discussed in the case appear to have little power in influencing the nature of the programme and little interest. However as, the key target market, the social marketer would aim to shift this stakeholder group by changing perceptions to move them to the B quadrant.

A final important stakeholder group comprises the various 'competitors' involved in social marketing programmes.

Competitor analysis

Hastings discusses the complexity of competitor analysis in Chapter 8 of the core text. Even for commercial marketers, competitor analysis is far from simple. Would Barclay's Bank have considered in the 1970s that Tesco would be a major competitor for some of its products by the end of the century? Deregulation of markets encourages new entrants whose core business may differ considerably from that of existing players. Competitor analysis involves a number of important questions for the social marketer. For example, to what extent is there potential for collaboration with 'the competition' and at what level does competitor analysis take place? For an example of competitor identification for a social marketing issue see box 4.1

Box 4.1 Identifying the competition for a social marketing programme: reducing obesity

Direct competition

Competing behaviours

These are the current behaviours which people are engaging in and which are the focus of the social marketing programme. They may be expressed as negative behaviours, e.g. eating unhealthily, or the converse of the positive behaviour, for example, not eating 5 portions of fruit or vegetables per day.

Competing benefits and motivation

These are the internal factors i.e. the physiological, psychological and other personal factors which people experience through engaging in the 'negative behaviours'. Over-eating can be a result of the need for a pleasurable experience and 'comfort-eating' is a well known phenomenon.

Personal influences

Other factors are external to the individual. Personal influences include family, friends, work colleagues and other peer group forces which encourage the individual to engage in competing behaviours. The role of peer group is a particularly relevant one for younger age groups and has an important influence on behaviours such as eating and exercise patterns.

Wider influences

Wider, impersonal influences include a wide range of organisations. A number of industries immediately spring to mind, for example, the fast food industry, alcohol manufacturers, retailers, and computer games manufacturers. These typically have considerable resources available to encourage competing behaviours through product development, branding and promotion. More recently, a number of these competitors have adopted 'social marketing' approaches in their product development and communications strategies, for example the healthier food options and promotion of responsible approaches to drinking. It is often worth asking whether there is a role for collaboration with competitors. The commercial sector often engages in strategic alliances with the competition, for example within the airline and car manufacturing sectors. Harnessing the power of commercial organisations can provide additional resources.

Indirect Competition

In addition to the direct competitors there are the myriad of other forces which compete for the target market's time and attention. These include:

Other social marketing messages

The particular target audience may be receiving a whole range of messages about desired behavioural change. This may distract them from the programme or build resistance to constant requests to stop behaving as they do.

Everyday life

When trying to attract the target audience's attention and engage them in the programme, the social marketer competes not only with all the forces above, but also with 'every day life. People have a limited amount of time and energy. Busy lifestyles and multiple commitments can underpin negative behaviours. Conversely, so can boredom and lack of financial or emotional security. Eating and drinking is an important part of every day life for many people as well as symbolic of special events – religious events and other celebrations. Changing established norms and values is a difficult process.

Wider environmental forces

Factors in the wider environment impact on the target audience and their everyday lives. i.e. socio-cultural, technological, economic, ecological, political, legal and ethical factors. The recent recession, for example, often focuses people onto lower priced 'luxuries' or treats, e.g. junk food.

Read Chapter 8 in the core text and try Exercise 8.2.

4.3 Market segmentation and targeting

Another of the nine key concepts described by Kotler and Levy (1969) is 'target groups definition'.

Market segmentation and targeting is at the core of marketing strategy and consumers (or potential consumers) are the key stakeholder group for both commercial and social marketers. In this section we focus on those specific consumers whose behaviour is the focus of the social marketing activity.

In Section 3.1 the factors which impact on consumer behaviour were outlined.

It is these factors – age, income, lifestyle – that are the basis for market segmentation. The process is as illustrated in Figure 4.4.

Figure 4.4 Market segmentation

Market segmentation is the process of dividing the market into groups of consumers who respond in a similar way to a given set of marketing stimuli, such as price or product features. Alternatively, groups of consumers/

customers with homogeneous needs or preferences will be divided into segments. This may be on the basis of demographics, such as age or gender; geo-graphics, such as country or rural/urban areas; psychographics such as lifestyle; or behavioural factors such as brand loyalty.

Subsequently the organisation will select a target market based on a number of factors. For example, will the target market provide the required level of profitability (or meet other objectives)? Will it be accessible to the organisation taking into account the available resources etc.?

The third stage is to position the product/organisation in a clear, distinctive and desirable place in the market (a) against competitors and (b) in the minds of the consumer. This is what Kotler and Levy (1969) refer to as 'differentiated marketing', which is achieved through product design, branding, pricing, promotional activities and so on.

An example of a market segmentation exercise developed for DEFRA (The UK government department for the Environment, Food and Rural Affairs) is shown below. This segments the market according to two criteria, i.e. *willingness* to act and *ability* to act in relation to sustainable consumption behaviour (Figure 4.5) and suggests seven potential target markets. Possible behavioural change for each segment includes:

Consumers with Conscience: use of 'smart metering' for more efficient fuel and water consumption.

Greens: reuse and repair consumer durables.

Wastage-Focussed: home composting

Currently Constrained: avoid high impact commodities

Long Term Restricted: increase recycling

Basic Contributors: plant for wildlife

Disinterested: none suggested

Clearly selection of target audiences requires identification of those groups where behavioural change is most likely in view of the available resource constraints, for example, those with a high ability and willingness to act i.e. consumers with conscience, greens and the wastage-focussed are the most likely to respond to new marketing initiatives.

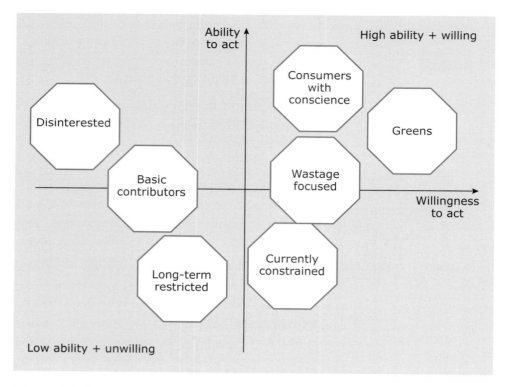

Figure 4.5 Sustainable Consumption Behaviour Opportunities

Source: Adapted from DEFRA (2007) *Survey of Public Attitudes and Behaviours toward the environment.* London: Department of the Environment Food and Rural Affairs.

4.4 Social marketing objectives

As with all planning processes, social marketing planning requires clear objectives against which to measure outcomes. The objectives of social marketing programmes will be in terms of behavioural change and their effect can be measured by, say, the numbers in the target market who quit smoking or the reduction in numbers who are prosecuted for speeding. There are a number of key issues which should be considered with respect to setting and evaluating the achievement of objectives.

- As Hastings emphasises in Chapter 4, behavioural change is often a long-term phenomena and should be considered as such when evaluating social marketing programmes.

- We should be clear that objectives, and their evaluation, are a direct result of the programme. In the speeding example below, a fall in numbers prosecuted for speeding could have resulted from a diversion of police resources.

- There will be a hierarchy, or system, of objectives which relate to each other. The objective of social advertising might be to create awareness of an issue and when integrated with other elements of the programme will achieve behavioural change. Similarly this will be part of a wider programme of activities, for example, part of a public health strategy and will feed into overall government and local government objectives and performance indicators.

Since many programmes are likely to involve public sector activity, objective setting will need to be framed within a prescribed set of performance indicators, for example in the UK the 'best value' measure is likely to play a role. ('Best value' is a measure which UK public sector organisations must apply to purchasing etc. The emphasis is not on least cost but value for money.)

- As discussed previously, the many stakeholders likely to be involved means that there may be a number of conflicting objectives that have to be resolved.

You will find further discussion of market segmentation and objective setting in Chapter 4 of the core text. Read Chapter 4 and attempt Exercises 4.1 and 4.2 which look at market segmentation issues and Exercise 4.3, which focuses on setting social marketing objectives. The second part of the chapter introduces the 'social marketing mix' which we will develop with reference to services marketing theory.

Activity 4.3

Read Case Study 3, 'A social advertising strategy to reduce speeding'. This focuses on both market segmentation and consumer behaviour theory, which we looked at in Section 3. Answer the three questions.

4.5 The marketing mix and the service element in social marketing

The marketing mix in social marketing

Once the target market has been identified, the traditional marketing approach is to develop a programme of tools that will result in the right product for that market; offered at the right price and delivered at the right time and place. Additionally, a communications programme must be developed that will make the market aware of the product and hopefully lead to adoption. Collectively, these tools are often referred to as the marketing mix or the 4Ps, i.e. product, price, place and promotion. These are the 'multiple marketing tools' referred to in Kotler and Levy's (1969) schema outlined in Activity 2.3. Together with the 'product' these combine to create the differential advantages which appeal to target markets. In Section 2.4 we also considered the nature of the social marketing product and asked what people were actually buying. We will now consider the other 'three Ps' within a social marketing context. You will already be familiar with some of these ideas as they are discussed in Chapter 4 in the core text.

(a) Price

With commercial marketing the role of price in consumer exchange is usually clear. The monetary cost is usually the main focus (although there may be other costs, e.g. opportunity costs and psychological costs involved). Monetary costs may also be incurred when adopting social marketing 'products'. Purchase of nicotine substitutes or healthier food, for example. Unlike commercial marketing, little or no cost (in terms of price) is necessarily endured by the actual consumer. However the concept of sacrifice, which is a key one in the consumer behaviour literature, is of substantial relevance and you will find many examples of this in the core text and case studies. Whatever the nature of the exchange, there must be perceived value by the parties involved. Zeithaml (1988, p. 14) defines perceived value as: 'the consumer's overall assessment of the utility of a product based on perceptions of what is received and what is given'.

Value represents a trade-off between the salient give and get components. Central to this is the give component of sacrifice – what is given up or sacrificed to acquire a product/service/idea. In addition to monetary cost, there are non- monetary costs of effort (including emotional effort), time and risk. Cronin et al. (1997) identify six sources of risk: financial, physical, performance, social, psychological and overall.

(b) Promotion

Promotion plays a major role in both commercial and social marketing. It is often the most visible element of the programme to the consumer and other stakeholders. As such, people often equate marketing with advertising. A number of decisions must be made and, as with all other elements of the marketing mix, these are determined by the nature of the specific target market. Decisions include – what type of communication to adopt; which media to use; the nature of the message and the method of evaluation. As this is a major focal area of social marketing we will look at this in depth in Section 4.6.

(c) Place

Place refers to the channels of distribution and encompasses the range of individuals and organisations (often described as intermediaries) who play a part in making the product available and accessible to the consumer. Many social marketing programmes rely on the delivery of messages and interventions through health, education and other services for their effectiveness. Consequently, social marketers will benefit from an understanding of the growing field of services marketing, which focuses on, amongst other areas, how consumers evaluate services and how service performance consequently impacts on their future behaviour.

The service element in social marketing

Consumers may encounter a range of services and service organisations in their experiences of social marketing programmes.

At one extreme the consumer may change their behaviour as a result of awareness of an issue, e.g. the health risks of a particular food (various health scares bear testament to this). At the other extreme this awareness may be generated within a service environment, for example, advice and follow up treatment by a hospital surgeon to change a patient's behaviour after a heart attack. Between these extremes are a range of examples, where a variety of organisations (commercial and non-commercial) become involved with the consumer in behaviour change. Consider changing behaviour for a healthier lifestyle. This may involve becoming a member of a gym and/or sports club; visiting the GP for advice and health-check; changing lunchtime habits from the fast food outlet to the health food restaurant as well as frequenting retailers for alternative foodstuffs, vitamins, exercise bikes and various instruments to monitor blood pressure, cholesterol, heart rate etc. Clearly, these producers are stakeholders in this example of social marketing. The main point here, however, is that if the various services (including retail) organisations do not provide the required level of service quality then the consumer may switch service provider and ultimately drop the behavioural change. In recognising the specific characteristics of services as opposed to tangible goods, Booms and Bitner (1981) have developed an extended marketing mix approach for services – to include people, process and physical evidence.

- **People** – One of the key features of services is that of 'inseparability', i.e. services are produced as they are consumed. Consequently service delivery often involves interaction between the consumer and the people producing and delivering the service and this will have a crucial impact on the way in which the service is perceived and evaluated by the consumer.

- **Process** – Process involves 'the actual procedures, mechanisms, and flow of activities by which the service is delivered – the service delivery and operating systems.' (Zeithaml et al., 2006, p. 27). The process may be complex and providers must therefore provide facilitating mechanisms. Helpful signage is provided in hospitals and leisure facilities. Use of technology also requires effective education of the consumer.

- **Physical evidence** – During the service process the consumer often encounters a variety of physical or tangible evidence, including the appearance of staff (which can provide important indicators and messages, for example of professionalism, approachability, cleanliness); logos, signage, graphics and correspondence; and the physical environment or service-scape. Zeithaml et al., (2006) describe how elements of the service-scape that affect customers include both exterior attributes (such as signage, parking, landscape) and interior attributes (such as design, layout, equipment, décor). The ambience of the service environment – music, smells, colour schemes – impacts on the mood of customers, their perceptions and consequent behaviour. The layout impacts on the degree and nature of social interaction and conveys messages about status and the consumer's role.

Initiating and sustaining behaviour change: messages and services

We have therefore identified two key players in achieving behavioural change – the message communicated to the target market and the services by which the product is delivered. Figure 4.6 provides some examples to illustrate how the relative role might differ according to the nature of the behaviour.

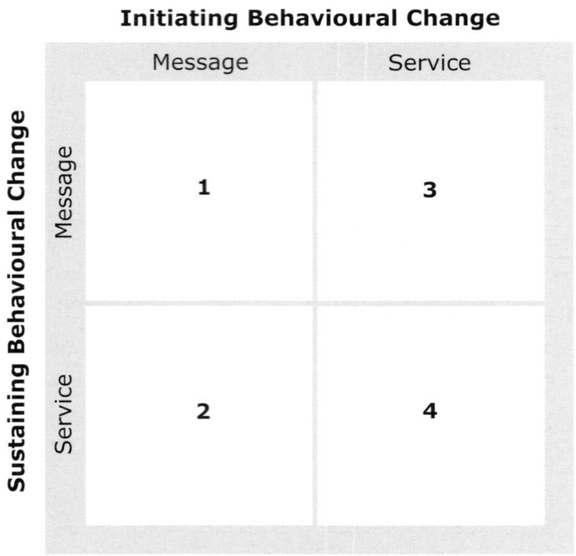

Initiating Behavioural Change

Figure 4.6 Initiating and sustaining behaviour change: Messages and services

Situation 1: The consumer does not come into contact with any services associated with the behavioural change. Messages may be personal (e.g. friends) or non-personal (e.g. media), for example, a documentary illustrates the benefits to the environment of not leaving electrical appliances on standby.

Situation 2: Behavioural change is initiated by the media (or personal sources) but these direct the consumer to services, e.g. lose weight, go to the gym.

Situation 3: Behaviour change is initiated by service and sustained/ reinforced by messages, e.g. a doctor suggests that a patient stops smoking: TV ads serve as a reminder.

Situation 4: Initiation and sustaining of behavioural change are both as a result of services, for example, a health visitor suggests methods of contraception and the family planning clinic provides and continues the service.

There are a number of implications of this approach. First, it suggests that the relative roles of non-service communication and service quality (which of course includes communication from the service itself) can differ in their impact on behavioural change dependent on the nature of the programme and its objectives. Second, it suggests the need for consistency between communication programmes and organisations/individuals involved in service delivery. Third it emphasises the importance of service quality and the findings of service marketing research to the field of social marketing. Finally, the analysis can be further developed to look at ways in which social marketing programmes may differ globally, for example, a differing emphasis where communications media may not be available in developing countries. Box 4.2 illustrates how poor service quality can impact on behaviour.

Box 4.2 An example of the importance of service to social marketing programmes: the case of family planning

The potential consequences of unwanted pregnancy (particularly for under-age girls) has been an issue for social marketers and others for many years. Additionally, the role of these services in the promotion of 'safe sex' is a crucial one. Effective family planning often involves a visit to a specialist clinic or general practitioner (GP). A number of studies have shown that the quality of family planning services can vary widely between providers. One study (Smith, 2000) highlighted the key factors which consumers evaluate as:

(a) expertise (particularly medical staff expertise)

(b) interpersonal qualities (both medical and administrative staff)

(c) convenience/access (including both time and place)

Of the 200 women interviewed in this study, 54 per cent had switched from a GP to a specialist clinic. Of those 39 per cent described themselves as mostly dissatisfied or worse (i.e. 10 per cent were unhappy and another 10 per cent thought that the service was terrible). In particular they felt that they were not encouraged to ask questions and that there was a lack of knowledge when answering questions. They also felt an unwillingness to help and a lack of understanding of their needs. This supports other studies where poor service quality has resulted in consumers either, as in this case, switching supplier, or worse, in switching behaviour.

Activity 4.4

i   Read Case Study 10 in the core text, 'Physicians taking action against smoking' and answer the questions.

ii How would a knowledge of services marketing help to develop the marketing plan for the final consumer market?

Comment

This case focuses on a social marketing plan to effect behavioural change in physicians and other healthcare professionals. Ultimately the aim is to change the behaviour of the consumer as a result of this increase in information and prescription drugs. Consequently a marketing plan will be developed for the consumer target market. From a services marketing perspective these professionals are the 'people' element of the marketing mix. They also represent an element of 'place' and 'promotion'. As such, consumers require a number of skills of them, including both expertise and interpersonal skills. A number of studies have highlighted the problems which patients encounter with respect to their GPs. One of which is a problem of communication. The case refers to 'reluctant GPs' and also to 'physicians perceived ability to communicate, listen and establish a relationship with patients. These skills need to be assessed, possibly through consumer research. In addition, the process should be assessed from the consumer's perspective, for example, how and when do they want this issue to be raised and addressed? Do they want it to be raised at all? Do they see this as an appropriate use of the GPs, and their time. This can then be communicated to the GPs to enable them to provide a good level of customer service. The final element is 'physical evidence'. The health associations of smoking cessation suggest that a doctor's surgery with its associations would be an appropriate environment. Again, however, this needs to be assessed by reference to consumers.

4.6 The role of communications and branding in social marketing programmes

One of the key tasks of social marketers is to develop effective messages which provide individuals with the information required to achieve behavioural change. Communication represents the 'transmission of information, ideas, attitudes, or emotion from one person or group to another' (Fill, 2002, p. 31). There are many models and frameworks available to help with communications planning. First, an understanding of how communication works is illustrated in Figure 4.7.

The linear model of communications

The communication process involves:

- the sender (source)
- the message itself
- encoding the message into a form which can be transmitted, e.g. written, oral
- transmitting the message
- the receiver
- decoding the message
- action.

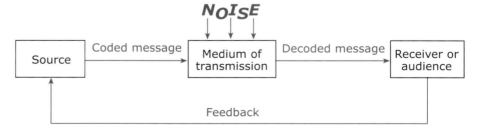

Figure 4.7 A linear model of communication

Source: based on Shannon and Weaver, 1949)

Evidently, effective communication involves the 'sender' of the message in encoding and transmitting the information in a way which is relevant to the target audience. Secondly, the receiver must have the ability to decode the message and to recognise the intended meaning. There should also be:

- feedback, which should ensure that the receiver has decoded the message effectively by responding to the message in some way.

A final element is:

- noise, anything in the environment which impedes the transmission and decoding of the message, e.g. conflicting interests, pressure of work, too many other messages.

Activity 4.5

Using the elements in Figure 4.7, list the factors which you consider may prevent effective social marketing communications.

Comment

Barriers to effective social marketing communication may include:

- Lack of understanding of the target audience by the sender. Consequently the message may be encoded using language or symbols which fail to transfer the intended 'meaning' to the audience. In Chapter 5, Gerard Hastings uses the illustration of an anti-heroin campaign where young people's interpretation of the results of heroin addiction, as depicted in the campaign, were favourable, rather than as intended, because of a lack of understanding of youth culture by the advertising agency.
- Inadequate definition of required feedback. The effectiveness of communication needs to be evaluated by the sender (campaign sponsors etc). Feedback may be defined in terms of actions, e.g. visiting a website or telephoning a smoking quit line. If no specific feedback is required then research may be conducted to assess, for example, awareness of the message.
- Incorrect choice of medium/media. Possibly because of funding constraints, or again because of lack of knowledge of the consumers' media habits, the incorrect medium or media may be chosen. Media may include impersonal sources such as television, newspapers, magazines etc. and personal sources such as professional services (doctors, teachers etc.) and peer group members, family etc. An important issue here is one of source credibility i.e. 'the extent to which a source is perceived as having knowledge, skill or experience relevant to a communication topic and can be trusted to give an unbiased opinion or present objective information on the issue', (source: Belch and Belch, 2009, p. GL3).
- Consistency of messages. In view of the many potential sources of communication it is vital that there is a consistency of message across the various channels. This is illustrated in the next model which emphasises the need for integrated marketing communications.

An integrated marketing communications framework

With a wide range of communications channels available to social marketers it is crucial that these deliver consistent messages. Belch and Belch (2009) describe the move towards integrated marketing communications as one of the most significant marketing developments of the 1990s. They explain that a fundamental reason for this is the recognition by businesses of 'the value of strategically integrating the various communication functions rather than having them operate autonomously' (p. 12). They adopt the American Association of Advertising Agencies definition of IMC:

> …a concept of marketing communications planning that recognises the added value of a comprehensive plan that evaluates the strategic roles of a variety of communication disciplines – for example, general advertising, direct response, sales promotion and public relations – and combines these disciplines to provide clarity, consistency and maximum communications impact.
>
> (Source: Belch and Belch, 2009, p. 11)

The basis of this plan is illustrated in Figure 4.8 (overleaf).

The integrated marketing communications programme is developed by reference to the various factors we have looked at in previous sections:

- The overall marketing plan including marketing objectives and competitor analysis.
- The promotional programme situation, e.g. internally – previous experience and ability with respect to promotions and – externally – consumer behaviour analysis, segmentation, targeting and positioning decisions.

And those we look at in this section:

- Communications process analysis – e.g. communication goals, receiver's response processes; source, message and channel factors.

Finally, the available budget and decisions with respect to budget allocation will input into the planning process.

Figure 4.8 illustrates six main approaches to marketing communications. We will now look at these in turn with respect to social marketing communications.

Advertising

Advertising can be defined as 'any paid form of non-personal presentation and promotion of ideas, goods or services by an identified sponsor' (Kotler and Armstrong, 2008, p. 426). There are many examples of social advertising in the core text. In particular you should note

- The use of the various media (TV, radio, newspapers, magazines).
- How advertising is developed for a specific target audience.
- The use of rational and/or emotional appeals; in particular the use of fear appeals to transmit messages.

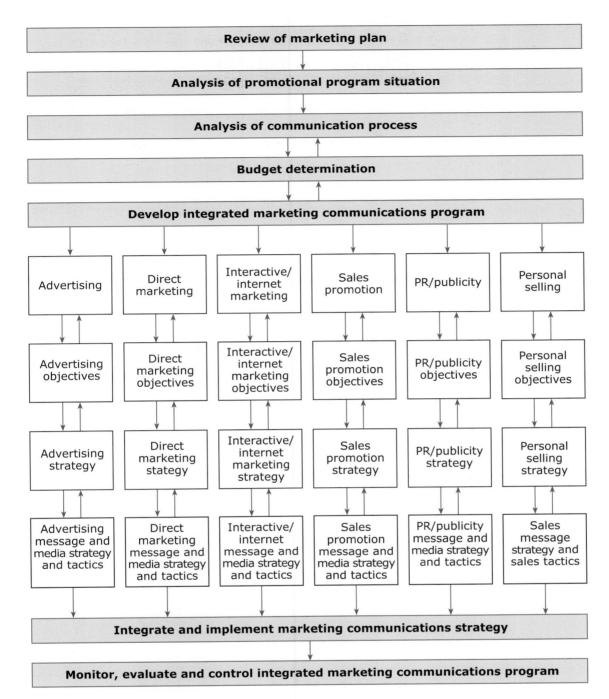

Figure 4.8 An integrated marketing communications planning model

(Source: Belch and Belch (2009: p30)

Direct marketing

This involves direct selling, direct response advertising, telemarketing etc. and is a rapidly growing medium in the commercial world. A particular reason for this is the growth in use of the internet as discussed below.

Interactive/internet marketing

Fill (2002) describes the internet as 'a distribution channel and communications medium that enables consumers and organisations to communicate in radically different ways'. Improvements in technology have dramatically changed the nature of communications and the ways of reaching target markets. This is particularly true of younger consumers which many social marketing programmes seek to target. The use of the internet as a complementary channel to television and other media was recently adopted in the UK in the 'Get Unhooked' smoking cessation campaign.

Sales promotion

Whereas advertising is traditionally associated with long-term brand building and can reach a wide audience particularly with the growth in global media; sales promotion is more often considered a short-term approach to generating sales. Promotional tools include introductory offers, competitions and point of sale promotions. These approaches can be readily associated with commercial sector organisations, for example, Boots (a UK retail chemist chain) is currently using in store posters to promote the benefits of stopping smoking.

Public relations/publicity

Similar to advertising, publicity is a non-personal form of communication but here there is no direct payment and no identifiable sponsor. Consequently publicity may also be negative, or adverse, since the organisation, group or individual may not be able to control it. For social marketers, publicity, negative and positive, often arises in the media as a result of scientific reports dealing with issues such as childhood obesity or environmental pollution. 'Media advocacy', which is a term derived from public health, is where the media are encouraged to cover particular issues and consequently communicate these to the public/and or specific target markets.

Personal selling

In the previous section, we looked at the importance of service organisations in providing information. As with all communication there is an issue of source credibility, and the credence which consumers, or potential consumers, give to a particular source is of paramount importance. The role of (health) professionals in many social marketing campaigns is an important one.

The communications mix – a few points to note

The above classification raises a few points that may be useful to bear in mind:

- Communication tools change over time and particularly as a result of technological developments.
- Related to the above point is a blurring of distinction between 'promotion' and 'place' (method of distribution). This is particularly true as direct marketing and subsequently internet/interactive marketing have been included as separate communications tools. It is also relevant to the personal selling element.
- It is also notable that, in addition to target markets of final consumers, communications (in addition to other marketing mix elements) must be developed for distributors (e.g. health professionals). This is often

referred to as 'push' promotion as opposed to the 'pull' promotion to the final customer.

Activity 4.6

Reading Read the article by Philip Kotler and Gerald Zaltman (1971) 'Social marketing an approach to planned social change', *Journal of Marketing*, vol. 35, no. 3, pp. 3–12. (See Appendix 2)

Note the following:

i   the discussion of the ideas of Lazarsfeld and Merton (1949), and Wiebe (1951/1952).

ii   the distinction which these authors make between social marketing and social advertising – and the argument as to why social advertising alone is not enough to effect behavioural change.

iii   how this journal paper provides a summary overview of the planning process covered in the previous sections.

How communications work

The paper by Kotler and Zaltman emphasises the crucial fact that, for both commercial and social marketers, it is the combination of the 'marketing mix' elements which will effect behavioural change. So what can we expect from communication and what objectives can be set for advertising and other elements of the promotional mix? In order to answer these questions we have to have some understanding of how promotion, and specifically advertising, works.

There are many advertising models and frameworks and they all have their critics. One approach is to focus on the stages which consumers move through as their attitudes towards the product develops. These are based on the attitude model which was discussed in Section 3.2.2, i.e. the cognitive – affective – conative model. See Figure 4.9.

- The AIDA (attention, interest, desire, action) model was originally designed to illustrate the stages which a salesperson should take the customer through and has subsequently been adopted as an explanation of how advertising works.

- The DAGMAR Model (defining advertising goals for measured advertising results) provides communications tasks which are specific and measurable using a four-stage approach, i.e. awareness, comprehension, conviction and action.

- Similarly the hierarchy of effects model (awareness, knowledge, liking, preference, conviction and purchase) is based on the idea that advertising will guide potential consumers through a number of stages which are essential if purchase (or other required behaviour) is to result.

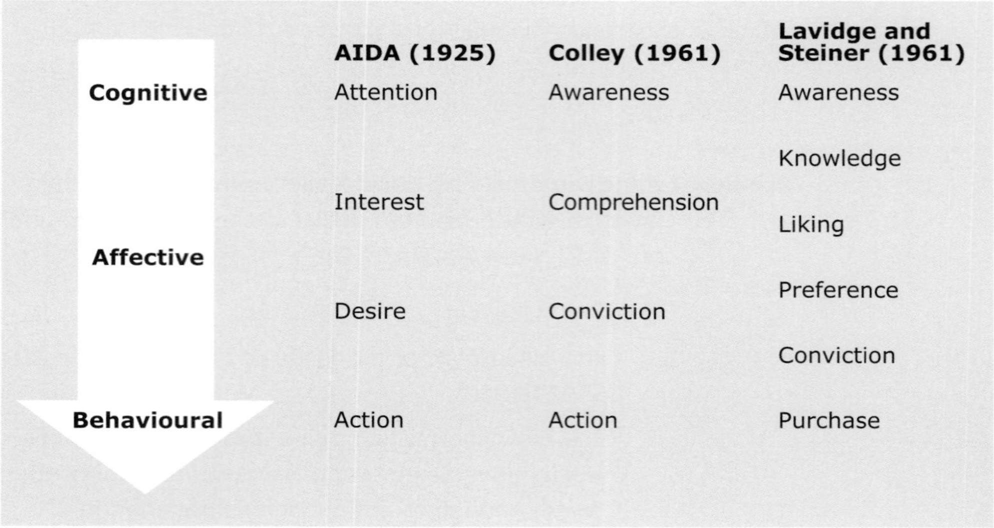

	AIDA (1925)	Colley (1961)	Lavidge and Steiner (1961)
Cognitive	Attention	Awareness	Awareness
			Knowledge
	Interest	Comprehension	Liking
Affective			Preference
	Desire	Conviction	
			Conviction
Behavioural	Action	Action	Purchase

Figure 4.9 Hierarchy of effects models

There are many criticisms of these sequential models:

- behaviour can precede the other elements of attitude for some decisions.
- a favourable attitude and positive intention does not necessarily result in purchase.
- the length of time which consumers take to move through the stages is unclear.
- how are these stages to be measured, e.g. how would you measure conviction?
- similar to the general criticism of the marketing mix approach is the focus on the consumer as a passive recipient of messages rather than one who will actively engage in information search and who is also likely to reject messages which are inconsistent with their current attitudes.
- later approaches to communication theory have added other sources of information which impact on the target market. In particular the role of opinion leaders and word of mouth communication from peer groups and others are important determinants of whether consumers will act on the basis of formal communications from marketers.

Although there are many issues in explaining how advertising (and other forms of communication) works and many other factors (e.g. the role of memory, the level of involvement with the product) have been included in subsequent models and examined in research studies – the sequential or stage approach can contribute to our understanding of the role of marketing communications. As with most theories and frameworks we have to ensure that the approach is relevant to the specific purpose and problem we are looking at and that we are aware of the limitations.

The role of brands and branding

Keller (2003) distinguishes between a 'small-b brand' as defined by the American Marketing Association:

name, term, sign, symbol, or design or a combination of them, intended to identify the goods and services of one seller or group of sellers and to differentiate them from those of competition

(Source: Keller, 2003, p. 3)

and the industry/practitioner definition of a 'big-B brand'. For the latter it is the amount of awareness, reputation, prominence etc., which creates the brand. The strategic role of brands cannot be over estimated. As described above, they provide the basis for differentiation. They also enable organisations to charge a price premium and act as a barrier to market entry for potential competitors. Some of the best known and earliest brands exist in those markets in which social marketers seek to intervene and change behaviour, for example, registration of some cigarette brand names, Dunhill, 1907; Camel, 1913; Marlboro, 1924 and Philip Morris, 1933. In the fast food sector McDonald's was established in 1937 and Burger King in 1954. By contrast some of the brand names associated with social objectives are more recent, for example, Friends of the Earth in 1969 and Greenpeace in 1971. Box 4.3 illustrates a social marketing brand which is gaining widespread awareness across the Europe.

Box 4.3 The Pan-European social marketing brand – HELP

The 'HELP, for a life without tobacco' campaign is built on an extensive programme of research and insight, with the aim to raise awareness around smoking prevention, cessation and passive smoking, particularly amongst young people, and to encourage a move towards tobacco de-normalisation. The first campaign was launched across all the European Union member states in 2005, with a second phase running from 2009-2010. For young people, a motivation to smoke is often the image of 'cool', 'rebelliousness' and of course 'fitting in with one's peer group'. This integrated communications campaign aims to change attitudes by portraying smoking as being 'absurd'. The main theme of the first campaign was to show people in typical smoking situations, but instead of a cigarette they were blowing a paper party-whistle, whilst the second campaign shows a young European's absurd tip on how to tackle a smoking issue, then leads the audience to real advice on the Help website. This interactive website (www.help-eu.com) acts as a relay for all media activities including the television and internet advertising campaign, press and media events. Young people can also share their own tips on the site. Since the campaign launch in 2005 nearly 12 million people have visited the website and to date nearly two hundred thousand smokers have signed up to the email cessation coaching service. Research shows a high level of brand recognition and impressive comprehension rates, specifically amongst the youth target.

For more information about the HELP campaign visit www.help-eu.com

Figure 4.10 Levels of relationships with brands
(Source: Belch and Belch, 2009)

Figure 4.10 illustrates how we, as consumers, have various levels of relationships with brands. At the base level we are interested in the product benefits. These are something which we think about and can be learned from advertising. Second, advertising can lead us to assign a personality to the brand. McDonald's is a good example. since their overt and very successful campaign led many people, and particularly children, to assign the brand personality of the cheerful Ronald McDonald to the company and its products. Finally, the consumer develops emotional bonds with the product/ brand. Belch and Belch (2009) describe how McCann-Erikson (one of the world's largest advertising agencies) has adopted this approach, believing that the creation of emotional bonds through advertising is essential to a positive psychological movement towards the product/brand and will reduce the potential for switching behaviour. Such emotional bonding with McDonald's could be achieved through the association with children's parties and happy family gatherings in which McDonald's staff and products play a part.

One question for social marketers is how to use the power of branding for social aims and objectives. Additionally, to what extent is the social marketer's role to break the emotional bonds we have with organisations such as McDonald's or to build bonds with social marketing brands?

Now that you are familiar with some of the basics of marketing communications and branding:

Read Chapter 5 in the core text and work through Exercises 5.1 and 5.2.

Note in particular the discussion of fear messages in social marketing programmes.

Activity 4.7

Now listen to the podcast – *Ethics and Advertising* by Gerard Hastings and Tom Farrell

In this podcast Tom focuses on the issue of fear appeals in social marketing. Tom asks – 'is it ever justifiable to use shock tactics showing violent images to promote social marketing messages?'

The debate centres around the issues of relationships, the complexities of behavioural change and the need for long term lifestyle change. The role of social marketing in developing and maintaining relationships with customers is highlighted. The ethical issues highlighted in Block 2 are also debated, for example negative emotions can be generated by fear tactics involving upsetting images and the potential associations can impact on audiences other than the target audience. A limited use of 'fear' e.g. to create attention is suggested. This is also relevant to discussions of social responsibility in Block 3, for example, the sometimes upsetting images of poverty included in advertising campaigns.

Activity 4.8

Read Case Study 15: 'Be well, know your BGL. Diabetes: Australia's diabetes awareness campaign' and answer the case study questions.

5 The social marketing network: moving upstream

In Section 4.2 we looked at the wide range of stakeholders who might have an interest in social marketing programmes and activities. So far (as is usual for most discussion of 'marketing') we have focused on the final consumer as the recipient of the messages and services aimed at positive behavioural change. It is now time to return to some of those other individuals/groups/ organisations who form, or potentially form, the social marketing network. This involves a whole range of organisations, and others, for the social marketer to engage with as additional target markets. This is a particular issue when considering both the policy development and service delivery aspects of social marketing, for example, influencing governmental bodies to implement legislation regarding food labelling or smoking bans; or GPs to offer consumer-friendly family planning services. In Case Study 10 we looked at a social marketing intervention which was targeted at GPs rather than smokers. Gerard Hastings refers to these as 'upstream organisations' and in Chapter 6 he asks the question – 'whose behaviour has to change?'

When developing a marketing strategy for potential/actual collaborators the same social marketing principles and practices apply. A fundamental question relates to the nature of the exchange; 'why should government introduce an environmental policy or a school allocate resources to prevent bullying?' To put it bluntly 'what's in it for them?' or alternatively, how can we achieve goal congruence between the social marketer and these upstream organisations to achieve behavioural change? Once we are clear as to the target market then mix strategies can be developed to persuade upstream audiences that a specific behavioural change will fulfil their own goals. Chapter 6 in the core text provides illustrative examples of these issues.

Read Chapter 6 and note the seven reasons which Hastings suggests for moving upstream with social marketing activity.

Attempt Exercises 6.1 to 6.4.

Note how Figures 6.1 and 6.2 in the core text build on the model which we looked at in Section 4.

Activity 5.1

Having completed the various activities in Chapter 6, stop for a moment to consider how social marketing programmes may differ when organisations are the target market rather than individual consumers. Then check your thoughts against the factors described below, which are often described to illustrate the differences between organisational and consumer marketing:

Comment

Complexity of the decision making unit (DMU)/buying centre

Although decisions within a consumer context may be the result of group (e.g. family) decision making, for example, the decision to change eating habits; the organisational context is likely to create a more complex DMU or buying centre. As such, it may be more difficult to identify and access key decision makers and influencers.

Expert buyers

Organisational buyers are more likely to have expert knowledge of the issues under consideration, for example, the contents of reports focusing on the impact of environmental change. Consequently, social marketers must take this knowledge into account when developing communications (the parallel in the commercial world would be the salesperson's need for expert product knowledge within the context of the buyer's business).

Rational economic buying motives and criteria

Organisational buying is often described as 'rational' in that there are likely to be specific criteria against which to measure decisions. It is for example, often illustrated that organisations are less likely to indulge in impulse buying and more likely to have prescribed procedures which may take some time to implement. Again the emphasis is on the social marketer being aware of the ways in which organisations and specific individuals conduct their business when developing their policies and procedures.

Politics, power and culture

Despite the previous comment, organisational politics and culture impact significantly on the decisions which individuals and committees make. These decisions often have more to do with political rather than rational motives and reflect the distribution of power and individual's ambitions and motivations.

Power dependency in relationships

Thinking in the field of organisational marketing has moved away from an adversarial perspective where buyers and sellers are considered to have competing objectives (e.g. buyers want low prices and sellers want high prices) to a recognition of mutual dependency. This is partly due to the fact that there are fewer buyers in organisational markets and relationships are therefore likely to develop between buyer and seller. Additionally, products and services are more likely to be customised requiring cooperation in new product/service development and a greater investment by both parties in the relationship. (N.B. In Chapter 8, Hastings discusses the issue of power and the need for equal power in a collaborative relationship).

Differences between consumer and organisational buying behaviour

The factors described above illustrate why the social marketing approach to upstream organisations (and individuals within them) is likely to differ from that of the consumer market. Relationship marketing strategies (see Section 6) which originally developed within an organisational marketing context, are more likely to predominate over the traditional marketing mix approach. Personal representation is a key element of the communication process. Understanding individuals, their organisational relationships and motivations is crucial to effective upstream social marketing.

6 Relationship marketing

The 'marketing mix' framework is a useful one for organising ideas about how to motivate the final consumer, upstream organisations and other stakeholders to change their behaviour in line with social marketing objectives. In recent times, however, there has been a comparative decline in the dominance of the marketing mix approach in both theoretical and practitioner marketing. A new paradigm of 'relationship marketing' developed from both organisational and services marketing. This was a response to the recognition that the marketing mix approach adopted a transactions orientation where the consumer was a passive recipient to the organisation's efforts. At the beginning of the 1990s Gronroos defined marketing as:

> ... marketing is to establish, maintain, and enhance (usually, but not necessarily, long-term) relationships with customers and other partners, at a profit, so that the objectives of the parties involved are met. This is achieved by a mutual exchange and fulfilment of promises.

(Source: Gronroos in Storbacka, 1997, p. 480)

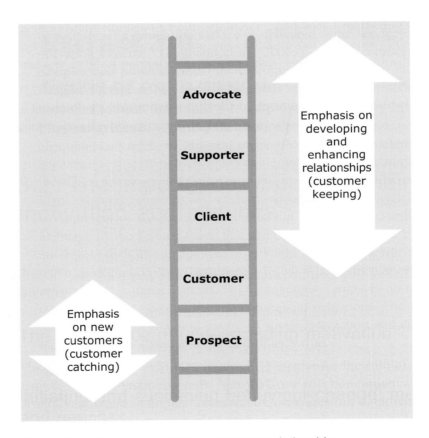

Figure 6.1 Stages in building a customer relationship

(Source: Christopher et al., 1991, p. 22)

A relationship marketing approach recognises the following underlying principles:

- It costs less to retain a customer than to attract a new one.
- Increasing competition increases customer power and the supplier must work harder to keep customers.
- 'Loyal' customers offer many benefits, e.g. 'cross-selling' – customers will buy a range of products. They will also attract other customers through positive word of mouth.
- The stages often described in building a customer relationship are shown in Figure 6.1.

For social marketers the benefits of a relationship marketing approach are clear. If relationships can be formed with stakeholders, this will potentially not only reduce the costs involved but also create advocates in both policy making and consumer groups who can act as opinion leaders and partners.

One final important point to note is that of the role of collaboration, cooperation, and particularly trust, in relationships. This is increasingly emphasised in many areas of the management and marketing literature. This is similar in many ways to the discussion of credibility when we looked at communication sources. If people don't trust the source of information they are unlikely to act upon it.

 Now read Chapter 7 in the core text.

Activity 6.1

Read Case Study 14, 'Using the internet to reach upstream and downstream in social marketing programmes' and answer the questions at the end of the case.

Consider the role of 'trust' in this example.

Comment

There are many definitions of 'trust'. These usually involve notions of reliance and confidence.

Young people trust the medium of the internet. In particular they perceive it, and themselves, as 'safe' which is important within the case context. Another important element is their confidence that their anonymity is assured.

7 The role of research in social marketing

The importance of research to building knowledge and planning and evaluating social marketing programmes is emphasised in the core text. The previous sections have outlined a variety of areas where decision makers and others would require information, for example:

- How would you identify target markets for a programme to encourage cycling as an alternative to driving?
- How would you determine the motivation/reasons for a negative behaviour such as smoking?
- How would you design and evaluate a promotional campaign for recycling?
- How would you assess the quality of services, e.g. for drug rehabilitation?
- How would you evaluate overall satisfaction with a social marketing initiative, e.g. reducing youth offending?

These are the sorts of questions which market and social research can help to answer. First, let us consider the what differences are between marketing and social research.

Table 7.1: Differences in emphasis between marketing and social research

Emphasis	Marketing research	Social research
External environment	Commercial	Society
Key focus	Customers and competitors	Stakeholders
Attitudes of interest	Attitudes towards organisations and their products and services	'Social' attitudes, i.e. attitudes to 'social issues'
Behaviour of interest	Purchasing decisions and shopping behaviour	How we live and behave in the social world
Commissioned by	Managers in profit-making organisations but increasingly those in not-for-profit organisations	Government departments, public bodies, public services, local government, non-governmental organisations
Purpose of research	Management decision making. Development of marketing programmes	Policy making. Development of social programmes. Resource allocation

Table 7.1 highlights some key criteria, many of which have been described by McGivern (2006).

Distinctions between the two approaches to research are not 'clear cut', however. Greenley and Foxall (1998) for example, have emphasised the need for marketing as a discipline to focus on all organisational stakeholders and not just customers and competitors. Additionally, although McGivern (2006) emphasises the role of research in resource allocation decisions for social marketing, this is also a key factor for commercial organisations. Within a social marketing context the two become even more similar as the research focusing on social behaviour will be used for the development of marketing programmes to include selection of target markets and development of appropriate services/communications. Definitions of marketing and social research will serve further to illustrate the similarities.

Definition of marketing research

The systematic design, collection, analysis and reporting of data relevant to a specific marketing situation facing an organisation.

(Source: Kotler and Armstrong, 2008, p. 100)

Definition of social research

The Social Research Association defines social research as:

the process of systematically gathering, analysing and interpreting information about the behaviour, knowledge, beliefs, attitudes and values of human populations.

(www.the-sra.org.uk in McGivern, 2006, p. 5)

7.1 Key issues in the social marketing research process

Broadly speaking, research, whether marketing or social, tries to answer the questions of why, who, what and how (including for quantitative research, the question of 'how many'). These questions should be built into the design of the research project.

Problem definition

First we must ask why we are carrying out research and why are we making the various decisions with regard to methods of data collection, sampling etc. The first stage in establishing the need for research is to define the social problem, or element of a social problem, which the research will address. At the beginning of this block a range of questions were identified. These would initially be identified as problems for social planners or other decision makers, for example the local council wants to reduce pollution and has identified cycling as one way of achieving this. They want to know how to gain the best return on resources by knowing who the target market will be. The researcher must now turn this social marketing problem into a research problem, research will be conducted to identify the factors which influence the choice of transport: how cycling is perceived and how this varies across consumer groups. Specific research objectives can then be developed.

These research objectives will focus on identifying the reasons why people behave in a particular way. In other words we will revisit the factors which determine consumer behaviour (and organisational behaviour for the upstream organisations).

The sample

Depending on the nature of the problem, the research may focus on any of the stakeholder groups involved. The population of interest will therefore be a group of individuals, or organisations, who will form the sampling population. In the cycling example, one population could be cyclists and another could be non-cyclists. Both of these groups might be defined by geographical area either by residence or road usage. The key issue if a number of cyclists and non-cyclists are to be questioned is 'how representative is the sample?' i.e. can we be sure that the answers which they give us represent the views of all other cyclists and non-cyclists in the area? Sample bias could arise from a variety of factors. For example, by interviewing people at a particular time of day or in a particular location, it may become an unrepresentative, or biased, sample.

Research design

The next set of decisions focus on what the research should involve. Research design may be exploratory for example. This usually involves qualitative research methods such as in-depth interviews or focus groups. Here we might ask groups of cyclists, and non-cyclists, to discuss the key issues involved. The findings from this could then form the basis of a questionnaire to be distributed to a wider sample. A second approach is to adopt a descriptive research design. This could involve the distribution of a questionnaire. The resulting data could answer questions such as – who cycles, where, when and for what purpose; reasons for cycling or not cycling to work or for recreation etc. Finally, causal research may be adopted. Basically, this tells us that one factor caused another, e.g. that the creation of cycle paths reduces the perceived problems of cycling. Causal relationships can be established through statistical relationships such as correlation analysis. Alternatively, experimental methods can be used.

Data collection and analysis

The final set of decisions focuses on how the research will be conducted, for example; will it involve the collection of secondary or primary data or both? Secondary data refers to data that already exists and has been collected for some other purpose. This may be internal or external to the organisation and may include previous research such as surveys of attitudes towards modes of transport; trends in sales figures for cycle retailers, etc. A key question relates to the reliability and relevance of the information. The researcher needs to assess the credibility of the source, the age of the data, any potential sources of bias, and so on.

Secondary data alone cannot usually supply all of the information required. Primary data collection provides new data that is specifically gathered for the research problem and objectives. This may include surveys of cyclists and non-cyclists, as mentioned previously (by mail, internet, telephone or personal interview); setting up a longitudinal panel of road users to assess trends over time or observation, for example, through a camera audit of road users. These quantitative approaches may be supplemented through qualitative methods. Alternatively, qualitative methods alone may be sufficient to answer the research question, particularly if the research is exploratory. Data analysis will then identify the characteristics of those who would be most likely to switch to cycling, how they can be reached and what will be the most influential message to achieve this. This may result in a number of alternative segments.

Read Chapter 9 in the core text and try Exercises 9.1 and 9.2. The chapter explains how market research ideas (pragmatism, multiple methods, decision-making focus, action research etc.) are adopted and adapted in social marketing research.

The remainder of this block considers the use of focus groups and projective techniques in greater depth.

7.2 The use of focus groups in social marketing research

Focus groups, and their role in social marketing research, are discussed in Chapter 9 of the core text. A summary of the uses and benefits of focus groups is shown in Box 7.1 below. You might find the Ss and Ms described by Malhotra (1996) below, to be a useful way of remembering their advantages and problems.

Box 7.1

Uses of focus groups

- In-depth understanding of attitudes/perceptions/behaviour...
- Insights into language/jargon.
- Development of research problems/hypotheses/measuring instruments.
- Understanding findings of other methods (triangulation as part of a multi-method design).
- Identify normative assumptions and range of opinions.
- Generating new ideas.
- Testing and evaluating, e.g. advertising copy.
- Public participation.

Advantages of focus groups

- Synergism – Synergy relates to 'the whole being greater than the sum of the parts'. In other words, a group of eight people are likely to produce more ideas, information, insights etc. than eight individual interviews.

- Snowballing – Is the 'chain reaction' which can occur as one participant triggers ideas, thoughts, memories in others.
- Stimulation – If the social interaction in the group is good then an animated discussion can be generated.
- Security – Being with other like-minded people in a group can generate feelings of safety and security. This is particularly important when discussing difficult issues such as drug addiction.
- Spontaneity – Unlike interviews (particularly structured) discussion can generate unconventional and unusual responses.
- Serendipity – Linked to the above. A free-flow of information can generate 'accidental' insights and ideas.
- Specialisation – Since a focus group can be expected to generate significantly more information than the same time spent with an individual interviewee, a more specialised (and therefore more expensive) moderator can be employed.
- Scientific scrutiny – Recordings and additional observers will add to the level of accuracy in the data and quality control of the process.
- Structure – A good moderator will build flexibility into the process so that important issues can be developed and built upon.
- Speed – Faster to collect and transcribe than the equivalent number of individual interviews.

Problems of focus groups

- Misrepresentation – Focus group participants are not a representative sample of the relevant population. Consequently the findings cannot be generalised.
- Misuse – Linked to the point above. The relatively small numbers involved should not be used as a basis for decision making without further research. The uses outlined in this box clearly highlight how the results can be used.
- Moderation – A wide range of skills is required for effective focus group moderation. As with many areas of research, it is relatively easy to moderate a focus group but exceptionally difficult to do this to a high standard. The moderator can introduce biases through their steering of the conversation, encouragement of individual participants etc.
- Messy – With many people often trying to talk at the same time it is difficult to analyse and interpret focus group data.
- Misjudge – Due to the features of this method, for example; problems of poor moderation, nature of the group, small sample size and the problems of analysis, focus group findings can be misinterpreted.

Projective techniques

One of the benefits of qualitative research techniques such as focus groups (and also in-depth interviews) is their flexibility of structure. This enables, for example, the use of projective techniques – i.e. 'An unstructured and indirect form of questioning that encourages respondents to project their underlying motivations, beliefs, attitudes, or feelings regarding the issue of concern' (Kassarjian in Malhotra, 1996, p. 178).

Projective techniques consist of an ambiguous stimulus which can be administered to a group or individual by the moderator/interviewer. Respondents draw/interpret, various stimuli. For example, respondents may be presented with a question – 'A person who throws litter in the street is someone who… ?'

Answers may include:

- does not care about the environment
- does not care about other people
- whose parents have not taught them how to behave properly
- cannot find a litter bin.

These various answers illustrate people's perceptions of the behaviour and their own experiences. It might also explain which respondents are likely to engage in the behaviour.

The above is an example of a completion technique.

There are a number of projective techniques and these can be categorised into:

- association techniques – these involve immediate responses to a stimulus, e.g. word association
- completion techniques – the respondent is presented with an incomplete sentence or story and asked to complete it in their own words
- construction techniques – these include approaches such as picture response techniques and cartoon tests where the respondent expresses their view of what is happening in these by telling stories, completing voice bubbles etc.
- expressive techniques – respondents are asked to relate the feelings and attitudes of some other person to a situation, e.g. role play or third person technique.

Examples of projective techniques are provided in Box 9.4 in Chapter 9 of the core text; the benefits and problems are illustrated in the box below.

Box 7.2 Projective techniques

The advantages/benefits of projective techniques include the following:

- Tap deeper subjective meanings/symbolism/emotions than other methods can achieve.

- Respondents less likely to rationalise than for a more directed question format.

- More highly related to behaviour as these are likely to reduce the likelihood of social desirability bias (see below).

- Many techniques to fit different situations and research objectives.

- Respondents may be more highly motivated to participate as these can introduce variety, interest and often humour into the interview.

The problems/drawbacks of projective techniques include the following:

- The results are open to a degree of subjectivity and interpretation. Interviewers/analysts may ascribe meanings to the data which may not be correct.

- As with all methods of data collection and particularly where there is a degree of subjectivity; the reliability and validity of the data will be open to question.

- Cost – relatively small number of respondents and cost of trained interpreter.

- Sample size and selection.

- Non-response – for example, some people may not be willing to participate.

- It may be considered unethical to try to elicit information in a way that is not transparent to the interviewee.

Problems of social desirability response bias in social and marketing research

Socially desirable responding (SDR) is widely viewed as the tendency for people to present themselves favourably according to current cultural norms when answering researchers' questions (Paulhus, 1991 in Mick, 1996).

SDR may arise both consciously and unconsciously and may arise through self deception, defensiveness, deception of others or impression management (Paulhus, 1991 in Mick, 1996).

This bias is a particular problem for social marketers since the typical research areas are those which Mick (1996) refers to as 'the dark side variables' e.g. alcoholism, drug addiction, sexual behaviour etc. and are particularly susceptible to SDR. As a consequence, data analysis may appear to identify relationships which do not exist (i.e. spurious effects) or alternatively, fail to identify relationships which do exist (suppression effect) or change the relationships between measures or constructs (moderation effect). In addition, because the tendency for SDR may differ between groups, e.g. by age or culture, it could make comparisons between the groups meaningless.

How can researchers deal with social desirability response bias?

SDR is a particular problem for self-report measures such as questionnaires. A number of ways of dealing with SDR have been suggested. These include indirect questioning (both structured and unstructured) (Fisher, 1993): for example the projective techniques described in the previous section. Additionally, numerous scales and indices have been developed in an attempt to detect SDR, e.g. the Marlowe-Crowne scale.

Activity 7.1

How might social desirability response (SDR) be an issue in researching the public's attitudes towards mental health?

Comment

Mental health is often considered a taboo subject. This may be as a fear of losing one's own mental health or the lack of understanding of the mentally ill or both. As Case Study 17 (below) highlights, most mental health work has been related to de-stigmatising mental illness problems. Therefore when asked to discuss issues of mental health, respondents may offer what they consider to be socially acceptable answers rather than their real opinions and fears. Consequently positive or neutral answers might suggest potential acceptability for a local mental health resource centre to be created in the local community. This may, however, not be the case when the project is eventually pursued.

Case Study 17 looks at the issue of mental health in a different way and relates a social marketing campaign to promote positive mental health. To finalise our discussion of research in social marketing, read Case Study 17 and answer the case questions.

8 The role of ethics in social marketing

The final chapter of the core text focuses on ethical issues in social marketing. Ethics may be defined as 'the science of morals, that branch of philosophy which is concerned with human character and conduct: a system of morals, rules of behaviour' – also – 'professional standards of conduct' (Source: Chambers English Dictionary, 1990).

There are a number of reasons why ethics should be a major concern for social marketers:

(a) The basic premise of advocates of social marketing is that its purpose is for 'social good'. In other words, as argued by John Stuart Mill, the emphasis is on the good of the many. There is also the critical element of social marketing where it is suggested that the marketing activities of some organisations can be considered unethical. Like Caesar's wife therefore social marketing needs to maintain an image of being 'above reproach' if it is to achieve trust amongst both upstream and downstream stakeholders.

(b) Social marketing tends to focus on areas where ethics and ethical issues traditionally predominate, for example; healthcare and environmental/sustainability issues.

(c) All areas of social marketing decision making are subject to ethical considerations. In the previous section, for example, we looked at the methods of marketing and social research that could inform social marketing decisions. Increasingly, research methods and their impact on respondents are coming under scrutiny. Indeed the new Market Research Society's Code of Ethical Conduct runs to a booklet of many pages. A link to the booklet is provided on the B324 website.

Activity 8.1

Read Chapter 10 in the core text. Make a note of any other reasons why ethical issues should be of concern to social marketers. As you work through this chapter, attempt Exercises 10.1 and 10.2 and note Figure 10.1, which should be very familiar to you.

---

9 Evaluating social marketing programmes

A crucial element of any social marketing programme is that of evaluation. Kotler and Levy's 1969 paper refers to the need for 'continuous marketing feedback' and emphasises that non-business organisations are typically more casual about collecting vital information on how they are doing. Certainly in the UK this has changed and a problem for many public sector organisations in recent years has been the proliferation of targets and objectives and the need to collect information to measure their achievement. However there are a number of types of evaluation which together provide essential information for decision makers and other stakeholders. These include:

- Formative evaluation
- Process evaluation – the implementation process
- Process evaluation – the planning process
- Impact evaluation
- Summative evaluation

9.1 Formative evaluation (pre-testing)

Formative evaluation is a continual input into programme design. It includes pre- testing individual programme elements such as promotional materials and service delivery approaches as well as the overall positioning of the intervention prior to launch. Aims of formative evaluation include:

- assessing the perceived nature of the exchange in terms of costs and benefits
- identifying appropriate messages, media, promotion methods and materials
- identifying their relevance to the target audience
- assessing the overall effects of the potential interventions on target audience
- assessing the effectiveness of each campaign against competitor activities.

Above all, formative evaluation generates a better understanding of the target audience and the actions which are likely to encourage positive behavioural change. A range of research methods might be used, for example, focus groups involving projective techniques as outlined in the previous section.

9.2 Process evaluation – the implementation process

Process evaluation focuses on the way in which the programme was implemented. It involves evaluating the opinions and attitudes of all stakeholders involved in the process. This will include an assessment of the success/failure of partner relationships, for example those between local health services, schools and retailers in encouraging healthy eating amongst school children. Aims include assessing stakeholder engagement and satisfaction with the programme and examining what did and did not work, and why. Methods might include a combination of qualitative and quantitative approaches to data collection from the target audience e.g. perceptions about quality of service, or a review of any local or national press coverage from secondary data sources.

9.3 Process evaluation – the planning process

A further element of process evaluation is to assess the planning process itself. This may be in terms of adherence to the social marketing planning approach outlined in Figure 4.1 and described in this wraparound. For example, was a detailed and effective stakeholder analysis undertaken; were specific and viable market segments identified; was adequate research undertaken into the needs, attitudes and motivations of the target market/s? In addition there will be an assessment of whether project objectives were achieved, (i.e. timescales, cost against budget and other resource utilisation measures), and how risk factors were identified and subsequently managed. Assessment will involve an analysis of secondary data such as minutes of meetings, reports, budgetary and milestone plans and interviews with key stakeholders.

9.4 Impact evaluation

Impact evaluation will focus on whether the programme has achieved the stated objectives and in particular, the behavioural goals. It is essential that objectives are clearly stated at the outset. These objectives must relate to a specific element of the programme and where a cause-effect relationship can be established. Unintended impacts/outcomes should also be assessed. Actual behaviour, knowledge, awareness etc. are compared to the targets set for the programme. For example, a programme aimed at reducing alcohol consumption may have included percentage changes in the increased awareness of the dangers of binge drinking; percentage reduction in alcohol consumption and an increase in positive drinking behaviours, such as switching to non-alcoholic beverages. Impact evaluation will involve collecting baseline data pre-implementation and post-implementation data for comparison. These measures could include: counting the number of free car park spaces after a programme to increase car sharing; the numbers who contact a 'quit-line' after a campaign aimed at smoking cessation. They are also likely to include more subjective self-report measures that relate to attitude change. The problems of self-report measures of attitudes and intentions, their relationship with actual behaviour were discussed earlier. One further issue relates to establishing cause–effect relationships. For this it may be necessary to adopt an experimental approach. This involves a comparison between the 'treatment group' (i.e. those people who have been involved in the programme) and the 'control group' (i.e. those who have not been involved or affected). Consequently any changes can be attributed to the programme and not changes in other factors.

9.5 Summative evaluation

The final element of the evaluation process involves a summary of the main learning outcomes and the benefits and limitations of the evaluation process itself. Summative evaluation provides an overall assessment of the programme against key criteria such as efficiency, effectiveness, quality and equity. It identifies the main factors affecting the success (or disappointments) of the programme; assesses the benefits/ limitations of the evaluation process in terms of timing, focus, content and usefulness of information generated; and explores areas where the greatest learning has been gained and how this can be exploited to its full potential. Methods include an examination of secondary sources, including previous evaluation data and interviews with stakeholders, particularly those stakeholders involved in programme design and delivery.

As the preceding process demonstrates, evaluation is an ongoing process which is essential to the success of social marketing. The main benefits of evaluation include:

- Assessing the achievement of aims, objectives and performance indicators on an ongoing basis.
- Providing information to relevant stakeholders on the results of the various elements of the programme and the programme itself. This will maintain positive relationships with stakeholder groups and maintain interest in future developments. In particular, funding bodies will require an assessment of the return on their investment.
- Providing vital feedback to inform the development and adaptation of the programme throughout the planning process.
- Providing the basis for learning from experience, both the process and the outcomes, of social marketing programmes including which elements, or combination of elements, appear to work and which do not. Feedback and evidence are essential for the development of more effective programmes and for determining best practice.
- Creating a greater understanding of the target market, for example, insight into the drivers and constraints of behavioural change which can be used for future programmes.

Activity 9.1

Consider a programme which aims to reduce the level of carbon emissions in a large organisation. The programme involves a range of activities such as team briefings; a promotional campaign to raise awareness and ideas forums to involve staff in creating innovative ways to change attitudes and behaviour so as to reduce carbon emissions.

How would you evaluate the programme (consider only impact evaluation)?

Comment

Measurement of carbon emissions against targets for reduction will be the overall and crucial measure. Changes in actual behaviour could be assessed by observation or self-report questionnaires. Similarly a measure of attitudes and intentions could be administered at various points in time. It may also be possible to set up a control group to establish whether changes are directly attributable to the programme. The various elements of the programme (e.g. the promotional campaign) can also be assessed against the specific objectives.

A final point relates to the timing of evaluation. It has already been mentioned that behavioural change is a long-term phenomenon. The programme may involve the stages of change approach which we looked at in Section 3.3 and therefore hope for staged improvements in attitudes, behaviours and therefore actual emissions. Conversely, the changes need to be sustainable, and therefore timed measures are essential to establish that the changes are sustained and people do not revert back to their previous behaviours once the initial enthusiasm has subsided.

Activity 9.2

Now listen to the podcast – Evaluating Social Marketing Programmes by Gerard Hastings and Michaela Firth

This second podcast with Michaela Firth from the UK National Health Service addresses how to evaluate social marketing programmes and interventions. Again, she asks questions which are of interest to practitioners.

Gerard emphasises the key role of research and the need to carry out various types of research such as formative, process and impact research. A second guideline refers to the need to set measurable and realistic objectives against which to evaluate various activities and the programme as a whole. Additionally, the need to control other factors is emphasised. Michaela also asks who should conduct the evaluation. Gerard points out the need for the practitioners who planned and implemented the programme to be involved, but also the need for objective evaluation involving independent commercial or public sector organisations.

Although the podcast refers specifically to social marketing, issues relating to evaluation are relevant to all areas of the module.

10 Conclusion

Now that you have worked through the module notes and the core text you might like to check back to the module aims and objectives and assess whether you feel that these have been achieved. Take a few minutes to think back to the two readings from 1969 and 1971. These still serve as a useful basis and framework for social marketing activity. However, significant developments in all areas of marketing have further contributed to our understanding of social marketing issues. These developments include: an improved understanding of consumer behaviour (through the substantial work since the 1970s focusing on the role of emotion in decision making) and the emphasis through the 1990s on the role of integrated marketing communications. Additionally, major theoretical areas, such as services marketing and relationship marketing, which developed throughout the 1980s and 1990s respectively, have provided new perspectives from which to view social marketing problems and solutions. A final source of learning has been from the many practical applications of social marketing interventions, some of which have been included as case studies in the core text. It is this combination of theoretical development and propensity for practical application which gives social marketing its potential to achieve important social objectives.

Do you agree?

Self-assessment questions

SAQ 1

Reading

Which of the following are not included as 'concepts for effective marketing management in non-business organisations' in the article by Kotler and Levy (1969)? Briefly explain why they were not included.

- Generic product definition
- Target group definition
- Differentiated marketing
- Consumer behaviour analysis
- Relationship marketing
- Differential advantages
- Multiple marketing tools
- Integrated marketing planning
- Services marketing
- Continuous marketing feedback
- Marketing audit

SAQ 2

(a) What is meant by 'social cognitive theory'?

(b) Why is it important for social marketers to understand this?

SAQ 3

What are the stages in the 'stages of change theory' (trans-theoretical model of behaviour change)?

SAQ 4

Is social advertising enough to effect behavioural change?

SAQ 5

What is meant by moving upstream in social marketing?

SAQ 6

Why might a relationship marketing approach to social marketing be more effective than a marketing mix approach?

SAQ 7

Effective social marketing communications require consistency of messages. Fill (2002) describes six elements which combine to produce an integrated communications programme. List the elements.

SAQ 8

What do you understand by the term randomised control trial (RCT). Why is this described by Hastings as an inappropriate research method for social marketing?

SAQ 9

Why might projective techniques be used in social marketing research?

SAQ 10

Why might it be difficult to evaluate social marketing programmes?

Answers to self-assessment questions

SAQ 1 Answer

Relationship marketing and services marketing are two aspects of marketing that have developed since the article was written. Both include important ideas, frameworks and tools, which will be of considerable use to social marketers.

SAQ 2 Answer

(a) Social cognitive theory describes how an individual's behaviour is determined by environmental factors such as family and friends; the individual's personal characteristics, perceptions of and interactions with the environment. An approach to adapting social cognitive theory to health behaviours is illustrated in Figure 3.1 in this document and is also discussed in the core text in Chapter 2.

(b) Social cognitive theory explains how people acquire and maintain behaviours. Social marketing programmes and interventions aim to change behaviour for the achievement of social goals. An understanding of the determinants of behaviour is therefore essential for the design of effective interventions.

SAQ 3 Answer

The 'stages of change' model identifies a number of stages which individuals pass through as they change behaviour. The stages are pre-contemplation (aware of the behaviour but not interested); contemplation (evaluating the personal relevance of the new behaviour); preparation (decided to act and putting measures in place); action (try the new behaviour) and confirmation/or maintenance (committed to the new behaviour).

Reading

SAQ 4 Answer

Both the core text and the paper by Kotler and Zaltman (1971) emphasise that social marketing is far more than social advertising. In both commercial and social marketing programmes it is the combination of all marketing mix activity which can effect behavioural change.

SAQ 5 Answer

Upstream organisations and individuals include policy makers, politicians, regulators, educators etc. This contrasts with downstream which relates to those whose behaviour change is the goal of social marketing activity. By influencing those upstream, social marketers can help to effect legislative, policy, attitudinal and behavioural change of key actors such as medical, social and educational workers, which will ultimately impact on the focal behaviours of the end consumer.

SAQ 6 Answer

Since the 1980s commercial marketers and marketing theorists have emphasised a relationship marketing approach rather than the traditional marketing mix approach. The former emphasised a transaction and the consumer as a passive recipient of marketing activity. The latter emphasises the (often) long-term relationship between producer and buyer and the active engagement of the consumer. The growth in services has helped to perpetuate the relationship marketing approach and its roots are usually described as originating in the organisational buying process. Consequently, a relationship marketing approach is particularly relevant to upstream marketing activity and also to where service organisations are involved in the behavioural change/maintenance process.

SAQ 7 Answer

The six elements are as follows:

- advertising
- sales promotion
- public relations/publicity
- personal selling
- direct marketing
- interactive/internet marketing.

SAQ 8 Answer

A randomised control test is an experimental research method which evaluates an intervention by comparing a treatment group (i.e. those receiving the intervention) with a control group (those who do not receive the intervention). The term 'random' refers to the statistical sampling of individuals to allocate to a particular group so that these are directly comparable. This is often used in medical trials and is also reflected in commercial marketing, e.g. test marketing of new products or advertising evaluation.

Hastings, however, highlights the costs and time involved; the complexity of human behaviour; ethical issues and the need to develop relationships with those whose behaviour is the target of marketing activity.

SAQ 9 Answer

Projective techniques include a range of approaches such as sentence completion, word association, psycho-drawing etc. they are described as 'ambiguous stimuli' and are used to elicit an individual's (often) repressed attitudes and motives. Individuals may not fully understand their own motivations and/or are unwilling to admit to them. This is particularly true of behaviours which are considered to be negative or 'anti-social'. Consequently people may not give true answers to traditional methods of questioning and projective techniques can help to discover true meanings underlying behaviour, The limitations of such techniques should also be recognised however, there is a degree of subjectivity in interpretation and poorly designed techniques may not gain meaningful data. Additionally, there are ethical issues to consider. Professional and ethical codes of conduct (see for example the Market Research Society's code mentioned in this block) usually consider 'informed consent' to be a requirement. Advising the respondent as to exactly what you are looking for will invalidate this technique.

SAQ 10 Answer

There are a number of reasons as outlined in the last section of this block. They include:

- Behavioural change is long term and so success may relate to attitude change or to progression through 'stages' (e.g. as per the model in SAQ 3) which may be difficult to measure.

- Evaluation requires that specific objectives are set in the early stages of the intervention and that marketing activity can have a clearly established cause–effect relationship. This is not always the case.

- Different stakeholders may evaluate the intervention in different ways. What is successful for one group may not be for another.

- It is often difficult to put a figure (e.g. 'value for money' or return on investment) on social marketing activity and therefore it may be difficult to create benchmarks for comparison.

References

Ajzen, I. (1985) in Chaiken, S. and Stangor C. (1987) 'Attitudes and attitude change', *Annual Review of Psychology*, vol. 38, January, pp. 575–630.

American Marketing Association (2004) *Marketing News*, 15 September, p. 3.

Andreasen, A. (1995) *Marketing Social Change – Changing Behaviour to Promote Health, Social Development and the Environment*, San Francisco, CA., Jossey-Bass.

Bagozzi, R. P. and Bunkrant, R. E. (1979) 'Attitude organisation and the attitude–behaviour relationship', *Journal of Personal and Social Psychology*, vol. 37, pp. 913–29.

Barr, T. F. and McNeilly, K. M. (2003) 'Marketing: is it still just advertising? The experiences of accounting firms as a guide for other professional service firms' *Journal of Services Marketing*, vol. 17, no. 7, pp. 713–29.

Belch, G. E. and Belch, M. A. (2009) *Advertising and Promotion: An Integrated Marketing Communications Perspective* (8th edn), New York, McGraw Hill.

Booms, B. H. and Bitner, M. J. (1981) 'Marketing strategies and organisational structures for service firms' in Donnelly, J. H. and George, W. R. (eds) *Marketing of Services*, Chicago, American Marketing Association, pp. 47–51.

Chambers (1990) *Chambers English Dictionary* (7th edn), Edinburgh, W&R Chambers Ltd.

Chartered Institute of Marketing (1997) *Dictionary of Marketing*, London, Kogan Page.

Cronin, J. J., Brady, M. K., Brand, R. R., Hightower Jr, R. and Shemwell, D. J. (1997) 'A cross-sectional test of the effect and conceptualisation of service value', *The Journal of Services Marketing*, vol. 11, no. 6, pp. 375–91.

Department of the Environment, Food and Rural Affairs (DEFRA), (2007) *Survey of Public Attitudes and Behaviours toward the environment.* London.

Fill, C. (2002) *Marketing Communications: Contexts, Strategies and Applications* (3rd edn), Harlow, Prentice-Hall/Financial Times/Pearson Education.

Fischbacher, M. (2005), 'Masters in public health', course material,. University of Glasgow, [unpublished].

Fishbein, M. (1970) 'The relationships between beliefs, attitudes and behaviour' in Kollat, D. T., Blackwell, R. D. and Engel, J. F. (eds.) *Research in Consumer Behaviour*, Oxford, Elsevier.

Fishbein, M. and Ajzen, I. (1975) *Belief, Attitude, Intention and Behaviour: An Introduction to Theory and Research*, New Jersey, Addison-Wesley.

Fisher, R. J. (1993) 'Social desirability bias and the validity of indirect questioning', *Journal of Consumer Research*, vol. 20, pp. 303–15.

Freeman, R. E. (1984) *Strategic Management: A Stakeholder Approach, Boston*, Pitman.

Greenley, G. E. and Foxall, G. R. (1998) 'External moderation of associations among stakeholder orientations and company performance', *International Journal of Research in Marketing*, vol. 15, pp. 51–69.

Gronroos, C. (1990) in Storbacka, K. (1997) 'Segmentation based on customer profitability: retrospective analysis of retail bank customer bases', *Journal of Marketing Management*, vol. 13, no. 5, pp. 479–92.

Hastings, G. (2007) *Social Marketing: Why should the Devil have all the best tunes?* Oxford, Butterworth Heinemann.

Kassarjian, H. H. (1974) 'Projective methods' in Ferber R. (ed) *Handbook of Marketing Research*, New York, McGraw Hill, pp. 3.85–3.100.

Johnson, G. and Scholes, K. (1999) *Exploring Corporate Strategy*, (5th edn) Prentice Hall Europe.

Katz, D. (1970) 'The functional approach to the study of attitudes' in Kollat, D. T., Blackwell, R. D. and Engel, J. F. (eds) *Research in Consumer Behaviour*, Oxford, Elsevier.

Katz, D. and Stotland, E. (1959) in Chaiken and Stangor (1987) 'Attitudes and attitude change', *Annual Review of Psychology*, vol. 38, January, pp. 575–630.

Keller, K. L. (2003) *Strategic Brand Management: Building, Measuring, and Managing Brand Equity* (2nd edn), New Jersey, Prentice Hall.

Kotler, P. and Armstrong, G. (2008) *Principles of Marketing* (12th edn), New Jersey, Pearson Education.

Kotler, P., Roberto, E. L. and Lee, N. (2002) *Social Marketing: Improving the Quality of Life*, London, Sage Publications.

Kotler, P. and Levy, S. (1969) 'Broadening the concept of marketing', *Journal of Marketing,* vol. 33, no. 1, pp. 10–15.

Kotler, P. and Zaltman, G. (1971) 'Social marketing: an approach to planned social change', *Journal of Marketing*, vol. 35, no. 3, pp. 3–12.

Krause, D. G. (1995) *Sun Tzu: The Art of war for Executives*, London, Nicholas Brealey Publishing.

Lazer and Kelley (1973) in Hastings, G. (2007) *Social marketing: why should the Devil have all the best tunes?*, Oxford, Butterworth Heinemann.

Lazarsfeld, P. F. and Merton, R. K. (1949) in Kotler, P. and Zaltman, G. (1971) 'Social marketing: an approach to planned social change', *Journal of Marketing*, vol. 35, no. 3, pp. 3–12.

Levitt, T. (1981) 'Making intangible products and product intangibles', *Harvard Business Review*, May–June, pp. 94–102.

Luck, D. J. (1969) 'Broadening the concept of marketing too far', *Journal of Marketing,* vol. 33, no. 3, pp. 53–5.

MacFadyen, L., Hastings, G., MacKintosh, A. and Lowry, R. (1998) 'Tobacco marketing and children's smoking: moving the debate beyond advertising and sponsorship', 27th EMAC Conference, Stockholm, May.

Malhotra, N. K. (1996) *Marketing Research: An Applied Orientation* (2nd edn), New Jersey, Prentice Hall International Editions.

Market Research Society (2005) *Code of Conduct*, December, Market Research Society, London

Maslow, A. (1943) 'A theory of human motivation', *Psychological Review*, vol. 50, pp. 370–96.

McGivern, Y. (2006) *The Practice of Market and Social Research: An Introduction* (2nd edn), London, Prentice Hall/Financial Times.

Meidan, A., Peck, M. and Handscombe, R. D. (2000) 'Marketing performance and business risk in Acutecare Health Trusts – a new comparative approach', *The Service Industries Journal*, vol. 20, no. 3, pp. 61–79.

Mick, G. (1996) 'Are studies of dark side variables confounded by socially desirable responding? The case of materialism', *Journal of Consumer Research,* vol. 23, pp. 106–19.

Shannon, C.E. and Weaver, W. (1998) *The Mathematical Theory of Communication*, Urbana, IL., University of Illinois Press.

Smith, A. M. (2000) 'The dimensions of service quality: Lessons from the healthcare literature and some methodological effects', *The Service Industries Journal,* vol. 20, no. 3, pp. 167–90.

The Market Research Society (2005) Code of Conduct [online] www.mrs.org.uk (Accessed 15 August 2007).

Turnbull, P. and Wootton, P.D. (1980) 'The bank manager: marketer, salesman or administrator' *European Journal of Marketing,* vol. 14, no. 8, p. 471–92.

Wiebe, G. D. (1951/1952) in Kotler, P. and Zaltman, G. (1971) 'Social marketing: an approach to planned social change', *Journal of Marketing*, vol. 35, no. 3, pp. 3–12.

Zeithaml, V.A. (1988) 'Consumer perceptions of price, quality and value: a means-end model and synthesis of evidence', *Journal of Marketing*, vol. 52, pp. 2–22.

Zeithaml, V.A., Bitner, M. J. and Gremler D.D. (2006) *Services Marketing: Integrating Customer Focus Across the Firm* (4th edn), New York, McGraw Hill International Edition.

Appendices

Appendix 1

Broadening the Concept of Marketing

Philip Kotler and Sidney J Levy

Journal of Marketing, January, 1969

The term 'marketing' connotes to most people a function peculiar to business firms. Marketing is seen as the task of finding and stimulating buyers for the firm's output. It involves product development, pricing, distribution and communication; and in the more progressive firms, continuous attention to the changing needs of customers and the development of new products, with product modifications and services to meet these needs. But whether marketing is viewed in the old sense of 'pushing' products or in the new sense of 'customer satisfaction engineering', it is almost always viewed and discussed as a business activity.

It is the authors' contention that marketing is a pervasive societal activity that goes considerably beyond the selling of toothpaste, soap and steel. Political contests remind us that candidates are marketed as well as soap; student recruitment by colleges reminds us that higher education is marketed; and fund raising reminds that 'causes' are marketed. Yet these areas of marketing are typically ignored by the student of marketing. Or they are treated cursorily as public relations or publicity activities. No attempt is made to incorporate these phenomena in the body proper of marketing thought and theory. No attempt is made to redefine the meaning of product development, pricing, distribution and communication in these newer contexts to see if they have a useful meaning. No attempt is made to examine whether the principles of 'good' marketing in traditional product areas are transferable to the marketing of services, persons and ideas.

The authors see a great opportunity for marketing people to expand their thinking and to apply their skills to an increasingly interesting range of social activity. The challenge depends on the attention given to it; marketing will either take on a broader social meaning or remain a narrowly defined business activity.

> Marketing is a pervasive societal activity that goes considerably beyond the selling of toothpaste, soap and steel. The authors interpret the meaning of marketing for non-business organizations and the nature of marketing functions such as product improvement, pricing, distribution and communication in such organizations. The question considered is whether traditional marketing principles are transferable to the marketing of organizations, persons and ideas.

The Rise of Organizational Marketing

One of the most striking trends in the United States is the increasing amount of society's work being performed by organizations other than business firms. As a society moves beyond the stage where shortages of food, clothing and shelter are the major problems, it begins to organize to meet other social needs that formerly had been put aside. Business enterprises remain a dominant type of organization but other types of organizations gain in conspicuousness and in influence. Many of these organizations become enormous and require the same rarefied management skills as traditional business organizations. Managing the United Auto Workers, Defense Department, Food Foundation, World Bank, Catholic Church and University of California has become every bit as challenging as managing Procter and Gamble, General Motors and General Electric. These non-business organizations have an increasing range of influence, affect as many livelihoods and occupy as much media prominence as major business firms.

All of these organizations perform the classic business functions. Every organization must perform a financial function insofar as money must be raised, managed and budgeted according to sound business principles. Every organization must perform a production function in that it must conceive of the best way of arranging inputs to produce the outputs of the organization. Every organization must perform a personnel function in that people must be hired, trained, assigned and promoted in the course of the organization's work. Every organization must perform a purchasing function in that it must acquire materials in an efficient way through comparing and selecting sources of supply.

When we come to the marketing function, it is also clear that every organization performs marketing-like activities whether or not they are recognized as such. Several examples can be given.

The police department of a major US city, concerned with the poor image it has among an important segment of its population, developed a campaign to 'win friends and influence people'. One highlight of this campaign is a 'visit your police station' day in which tours are conducted to show citizens the daily operations of the police department, including the crime laboratories, police line-ups and cells. The police department also sends officers to speak at public schools and carries out a number of other activities to improve its community relations.

Most museum directors interpret their primary responsibility as 'the proper presentation of an artistic heritage for posterity'. [1](April 1, 1968), p. 55. As a result, for many people museums are cold marble mausoleums that house miles of relics that soon give way to yawns and tired feet. Although museum attendance in the United States advances each year, a large number of citizens are uninterested in museums. Is this indifference due to failure in the manner of presenting what museums have to offer? This nagging question led to the new director of the Metropolitan Museum of Art to broaden the museum's appeal through sponsoring contemporary art shows and 'happenings'. His marketing philosophy of museum management led to substantial increases in the Met's attendance.

The public school system in Oklahoma City sorely needed more public support and funds to prevent a deterioration of facilities and exodus of teachers. It recently resorted to television programming to dramatize the work the public schools were doing to fight the high school dropout problem, to develop new teaching techniques and to enrich the children. Although an expensive medium, television quickly reached large numbers of parents whose response and interest were tremendous.

Nations also resort to international marketing campaigns to get across important points about themselves to the citizens of other countries. The junta of Greek colonels who seized power in Greece in 1967 found the international publicity surrounding their cause to be extremely unfavorable and potentially disruptive of international recognition. They hired a major New York public relations firm and soon full-page newspaper ads appeared carrying the headline 'Greece Was Saved From Communism', detailing in small print why the takeover was necessary for the stability of Greece and the world.[2]

An anti-cigarette group in Canada is trying to press the Canadian legislature to ban cigarettes on the grounds that they are harmful to health. There is widespread support for this cause but the organization's funds are limited, particularly measured against the huge advertising resources of the cigarette industry. The group's problem is to find effective ways to make a little money go a long way in persuading influential legislators of the need for discouraging cigarette consumption. This group has come up with several ideas for marketing anti-smoking to Canadians, including television spots, a paperback book featuring pictures of cancer and heart disease patients and legal research on company liability for the smoker's loss of health.

What concepts are common to these and many other possible illustrations of organizational marketing? All of these organizations are concerned about their 'product' in the eyes of certain 'consumers' and are seeking to find 'tools' for furthering their acceptance. Let us consider each of these concepts in general organizational terms.

Products

Every organization produces a 'product' of at least one of the following types:

Physical products. 'Product' first brings to mind everyday items like soap, clothes and food, and extends to cover millions of *tangible* items that have a market value and are available for purchase.

Services. Services are *intangible* goods that are subject to market transaction such as tours, insurance, consultation, hairdos and banking.

Persons. Personal marketing is an endemic *human* activity, from the employee trying to impress his boss to the statesman trying to win the support of the public. With the advent of mass communications, the marketing of persons has been turned over to professionals. Hollywood stars have their press agents, political candidates, their advertising agencies, and so on.

Organizations. Many organizations spend a great deal of time marketing themselves. The Republican Party has invested considerable thought and resources in trying to develop a modern look. The American Medical Association decided recently that it needed to launch a campaign to improve the image of the American doctor.[3] Many charitable organizations and universities see selling their *organization* as their primary responsibility.

Ideas. Many organizations are mainly in the business of selling *ideas* to the larger society. Population organizations are trying to sell the idea of birth control, and the Women's Christian Temperance Union is still trying to sell the idea of prohibition.

Thus the 'product' can take many forms, and this is the first crucial point in the case for broadening the concept of marketing.

Consumers

The second crucial point is that organizations must deal with many groups that are interested in their products and can make a difference in its success. It is vitally important to the organization's success that it be sensitive to, serve and satisfy these groups. One set of groups can be called the *suppliers*. *Suppliers* are those who provide the management group with the inputs necessary to perform its work and develop its product effectively. Suppliers include employees, vendors of the materials, banks, advertising agencies and consultants.

The other set of groups are the *consumers* of the organization's product, of which four sub-groups can be distinguished. The *clients* are those who are the immediate consumers of the organization's product. The clients of a business firm are its buyers and potential buyers; of a service organization those receiving the services, such as the needy (from the Salvation Army) or the sick (from County Hospital); and of a protective or a primary organization, the members themselves. The second group is the *trustee* or *directors*, those who are vested with the legal authority and responsibility for the organization, oversee the management, and enjoy a variety of benefits from the 'product'. The third group is the active *publics* that take a specific interest in the organization. For a business firm, the active publics include consumer rating groups, governmental agencies, and pressure groups of various kinds. For a university, the active publics include alumni and friends of the university, foundations, and city fathers. Finally, the fourth consumer group is the *general public*. These are all the people who might develop attitudes toward the organization that might affect its conduct in some way. Organizational marketing concerns the programs designed by management to create satisfactions and favorable attitudes in the organization's four consuming groups: clients, trustees, active publics, and general public.

Marketing Tools

Students of business firms spend much time studying the various tools under the firm's control that affect product acceptance: product improvement, pricing, distribution, and communication. All of these tools have counterpart applications to non-business organizational activity.

Non-business organizations to various degrees engage in product improvement, especially when they recognize the competition they face from other organizations. Thus, over the years churches have added a host of nonreligious activities to their basic religious activities to satisfy members seeking other bases of human fellowship. Universities keep updating their curricula and adding new student services in an attempt to make the educational experience relevant to the students. Where they have failed to do this, students have sometimes organized their own courses and publications, or have expressed their dissatisfaction in organized protest. Government agencies such as license bureaus, police forces, and taxing bodies are often not responsive to the public because of monopoly status; but even here citizens have shown an increasing readiness to protest mediocre services, and more alert bureaucracies have shown a growing interest in reading the user's needs and developing the required product services.

All organizations face the problem of pricing their products and services so that they cover costs. Churches charge dues, universities charge tuition, governmental agencies charge fees, fund-raising organizations send out bills. Very often specific product charges are not sufficient to meet the organization's budget, and it must rely on gifts and surcharges to make up the difference. Opinions vary as to how much the users should be charged for the individual services and how much should be made up through general collection. If the university increases its tuition, it will have to face losing some students and putting more students on scholarship. If the hospital raises its charges to cover rising costs and additional services, it may provoke a reaction from the community. All organizations face complex pricing issues although not all of them understand good pricing practice.

Distribution is a central concern to the manufacturer seeking to make his goods conveniently accessible to buyers. Distribution also can be an important marketing decision area for non-business organizations. A city's public library has to consider the best means of making its books available to the public. Should it establish one large library with an extensive collection of books, or several neighborhood branch libraries with duplication of books? Should it use bookmobiles that bring the books to the customers instead of relying exclusively on the customers coming to the books? Should it distribute through school libraries? Similarly the police department of a city must think through the problem of distributing its protective services efficiently through the community. It has to determine how much protective service to allocate to different neighborhoods; the respective merits of squad cars, motorcycles, and foot patrolmen; and the positioning of emergency phones.

Customer communication is an essential activity of all organizations although many non-marketing organizations often fail to accord it the importance it deserves. Managements of many organizations think they have fully met their communication responsibilities by setting up advertising and/ or public relations departments. They fail to realize that *everything about an organization talks*. Customers form impressions of an organization from its physical facilities, employees, officers, stationery, and a hundred other company surrogates. Only when this is appreciated do the members of the organization recognize that they all are in marketing, whatever else they do. With this understanding they can assess realistically the impact of their activities on the consumers.

Concepts for Effective Marketing Management in Non-business Organizations

Although all organizations have products, markets, and marketing tools, the art and science of effective marketing management have reached their highest state of development in the business type of organization. Business organizations depend on customer goodwill for survival and have generally learned how to sense and cater to their needs effectively. As other types of organizations recognize their marketing roles, they will turn increasingly to the body of marketing principles worked out by business organizations and adapt them to their own situations.

What are the main principles of effective marketing management as they appear in most forward-looking business organizations? Nine concepts stand out as crucial in guiding the marketing effort of a business organization.

Generic Product Definition

Business organizations have increasingly recognized the value of placing a broad definition on their products, one that emphasizes the basic customer need(s) being served. A modern soap company recognizes that its basic product is cleaning, not soap; a cosmetics company sees its basic product as beauty or hope, not lipsticks and makeup; a publishing company sees its basic product as information, not books.

The same need for a broader definition of its business is incumbent upon non-business organizations if they are to survive and grow. Churches at one time tended to define their product narrowly as that of producing religious services for members. Recently, most churchmen have decided that their basic product is human fellowship There was a time when educators said that their product was the three R's. Now most of them define their product as education for the whole man. They try to serve the social, emotional, and political needs of young people in addition to intellectual needs.

Target Groups Definition

A generic product definition usually results in defining a very wide market, and it is then necessary for the organizations, because of limited resources, to limit its product offering to certain clearly defined groups within the market. Although the generic product of an automobile company is transportation, the company typically sticks to cars, trucks, and buses, and stays away from bicycles, airplanes, and steamships. Furthermore, the manufacturer does not produce every size and shape of car but concentrates on producing a few major types to satisfy certain substantial and specific parts of the market.

In the same way, non-business organizations have to define their target groups carefully. For example, in Chicago the YMCA defines its target groups as men, women and children who want recreational opportunities and are willing to pay $20 or more a year for them. The Chicago Boys Club, on the other hand, defines its target group as poorer boys within the city boundaries who are in want of recreational facilities and can pay $1 a year.

Differentiated Marketing

When a business organization sets out to serve more than one target group, it will be maximally effective by differentiating its product offerings and communications. This is also true for non-business organizations. Fund-raising organizations have recognized the advantage of treating clients, trustees, and various publics in different ways. These groups require differentiated appeals and frequency of solicitation. Labor unions find that they must address different messages to different parties rather than one message to all parties. To the company they may seem unyielding, to the conciliator they may appear willing to compromise, and to the public they seek to appear economically exploited.

Customer Behavior Analysis

Business organizations are increasingly recognizing that customer needs and behavior are not obvious without formal research and analysis; they cannot rely on impressionistic evidence. Soap companies spend hundreds of thousands of dollars each year researching how Mrs Housewife feels about her laundry, how, when, and where she does her laundry, and what she desires of a detergent.

Fund raising illustrates how an industry has benefited by replacing stereotypes of donors with studies of why people contribute to causes. Fund raisers have learned that people give because they are getting something. Many give to community chests to relieve a sense of guilt because of their elevated state compared to the needy. Many give to medical charities to relieve a sense of fear that they may be struck by a disease whose cure has not yet been found. Some give to feel pride. Fund raisers have stressed the importance of identifying the motives operating in the marketplace of givers as a basis for planning drives.

Differential Advantages

In considering different ways of reaching target groups, an organization is advised to think in terms of seeking a differential advantage. It should consider what elements in its reputation or resources can be exploited to create a special value in the minds of its potential customers. In the same way Zenith has built a reputation for quality and International Harvester a reputation for service, a non-business organization should base its case on some dramatic value that competitive organizations lack. The small island of Nassau can compete against Miami for the tourist trade by advertising the greater dependability of its weather; the Heart Association can compete for funds against the Cancer Society by advertising the amazing strides made in heart research.

Multiple Marketing Tools

The modern business firm relies on a multitude of tools to sell its product, including product improvement, consumer and dealer advertising, salesman incentive programs, sales promotions, contests, multiple-size offerings, and so forth. Likewise non-business organizations also can reach their audiences in a variety of ways. A church can sustain the interest of its members through discussion groups, newsletters, news releases, campaign drives, annual reports, and retreats. Its 'salesmen' include the religious head, the board members, and the present members in terms of attracting potential members. Its advertising includes announcements of weddings, births and deaths, religious pronouncements, and newsworthy developments.

Integrated Marketing Planning

The multiplicity of available marketing tools suggests the desirability of overall coordination so that these tools do not work at cross purposes. Over time, business firms have placed under a marketing vice-president activities that were previously managed in a semi-autonomous fashion, such as sales, advertising, and marketing research. Non-business organizations typically have not integrated their marketing activities. Thus, no single officer in the typical university is given total responsibility for studying the needs and attitudes of clients, trustees, and publics, and undertaking the necessary product development and communications programs to serve these groups. The university administration instead includes a variety of 'marketing' positions such as dean of students, director of alumni affairs, director of public relations, and director of development; coordination is often poor.

Continuous Marketing Feedback

Business organizations gather continuous information about changes in the environment and about their own performance. They use their salesmen, research department, specialized research services, and other means to check on the movement of goods, actions of competitors, and feelings of customers to make sure they are progressing along satisfactory lines. Non-business organizations typically are more casual about collecting vital information on how they are doing and what is happening in the market-place. Universities have been caught off guard by underestimating the magnitude of student grievance and unrest, and so have major cities underestimated the degree to which they were failing to meet the needs of important minority constituencies.

Marketing Audit

Change is a fact of life, although it may proceed almost invisibly on a day-to-day basis. Over a long stretch of time it might be so fundamental as to threaten organizations that have not provided for periodic re-examinations of their purposes. Organizations can grow set in their ways and unresponsive to new opportunities or problems. Some great American companies are no longer with us because they did not change definitions of their businesses, and their products lost relevance in a changing world. Political parties become unresponsive after they enjoy power for a while and every so often experience a major upset. Many union leaders grow insensitive to new needs and problems until one day they find themselves out of office. For an organization to remain viable, its management must provide for periodic audits of its objectives, resources, and opportunities. It must re-examine its basic business, target groups, differential advantage, communication channels, and messages in the light of current trends and needs. It might recognize when change is needed and make it before it is too late.

Is Organizational Marketing a Socially Useful Activity?

Modern marketing has two different meanings in the minds of people who use the term. One meaning of marketing conjures up the terms selling influencing, persuading. Marketing is seen as a huge and increasingly dangerous technology, making it possible to sell persons on buying things, propositions, and causes they either do not want or which are bad for them. This was the indictment in Vance Packard's *Hidden Persuaders* and numerous other social criticisms, with the net effect that a large number of persons think of marketing as immoral or entirely self-seeking in its fundamental premises. They can be counted on to resist the idea of organizational marketing as so much 'Madison Avenue'.

The other meaning of marketing unfortunately is weaker in the public mind; it is the concept of sensitively *serving and satisfying human needs*. This was the great contribution of the marketing concept that was promulgated in the 1950s, and that concept now counts many business firms as its practitioners. The marketing concept holds that the problem of all business firms in an age of abundance is to develop customer loyalties and satisfaction, and the key to this problem is to focus on the customer's needs.[4] Perhaps the short-run problem of business firms is to sell people on buying the existing products, but the long-run problem is clearly to create the products that people need. By this recognition that effective marketing requires a consumer orientation instead of a product orientation, marketing has taken a new lease of life and tied its economic activity to a higher social purpose.

It is this second side of marketing that provides a useful concept for all organizations. All organizations are formed to serve the interest of particular groups: hospitals serve the sick, schools serve the students, governments serve the citizens, and labor unions serve the members. In the course of evolving, many organizations lose sight of their original mandate, grow hard, and become self-serving. The bureaucratic mentality begins to dominate the original service mentality. Hospitals may become perfunctory in their handling of patients, schools treat their students as nuisances, city bureaucrats behave like petty tyrants toward the citizens, and labor unions try to run instead of serve their members. All of these actions tend to build frustration in the consuming groups. As a result some withdraw meekly from these organizations, accept frustration as part of their condition, and find their satisfaction elsewhere. This used to be the common reaction of ghetto Negroes and college students in the face of indifferent city and university bureaucracies. But new possibilities have arisen, and now the same consumers refuse to withdraw so readily. Organized dissent and protest are seen to be an answer, and many organizations thinking of themselves as responsible have been stunned into recognizing that they have lost touch with their constituencies. They had grown unresponsive.

Where does marketing fit into this picture? Marketing is that function of the organization that can keep in constant touch with the organization's consumers, read their needs, develop 'products' that meet these needs, and build a program of communications to express the organization's purposes. Certainly selling and influencing will be large parts of organizational marketing; but, properly seen, selling follows rather than precedes the organization's drive to create products to satisfy its consumers.

Conclusion

It has been argued here that the modern marketing concept serves very naturally to describe an important facet of all organizational activity. All organizations must develop appropriate products to serve their sundry consuming groups and must use modern tools of communication to reach their consuming publics. The business heritage of marketing provides a useful set of concepts for guiding all organizations.

The choice facing those who manage non-business organizations is not whether to market or not to market, for no organization can avoid marketing. The choice is whether to do it well or poorly, and on this necessity the case for organizational marketing is basically founded.

ABOUT THE AUTHORS. Philip Kotler is Professor of Marketing at North-western University. He earned his PhD at M.I.T. He is the author of *Marketing Management: Analysis, Planning and Control.* Professor Kotler is Advisory Editor of the Holt, Rinehart and Winston Marketing Series and is an active consultant to many companies on marketing planning and information systems. Currently he is Chairman of the College on Marketing of The institute of Management Sciences.

Sidney J Levy is Professor of Marketing at Northwestern University and is Vice President of Social Research, Inc. He earned his PhD at the University of Chicago. Professor Levy is author of *Promotion: A Behavioral View,* co-author of *Living with Television,* and of many articles.

Kotler, P. and Levy, S. J (1969) *Journal of Marketing,* vol. 33, no. 1, pp. 10–15

[1] This is the view of Sherman Lee, Director of the Cleveland Museum, quoted in *Newsweek,* Vol. 71

[2] 'PR for the Colonels', *Newsweek,* Vol. 71 (March 18, 1968), p. 70.

[3] 'Doctors Try an Image Transplant', *Business Week,* No. 2025 (June 22, 1968), p. 64.

[4] Theodore Levitt, 'Marketing Myopia', *Harvard Business Review,* Vol. 38 (July-August, 1960), pp. 45-56.

Appendix 2

Social Marketing: An Approach to Planned Social Change

Philip Kotler and Gerald Zaltman

Journal of Marketing, July, 1971

In 1952, G. D. Wiebe raised the question 'Why can't you sell brotherhood like you sell soap?'[1] This statement implies that sellers of commodities such as soap are generally effective, while 'sellers' of social causes are generally ineffective. Wiebe examined four social campaigns to determine what conditions or characteristics accounted for their relative success or lack of success. He found that the more the conditions of the social campaign resembled those of a product campaign, the more successful the social campaign. However, because many social campaigns are conducted under quite un-market-like circumstances, Wiebe also noted clear limitations in the practice of social marketing.

A different view is implied in Joe McGinniss's best-selling book *The Selling of a President 1968.*[2] It's theme seems to be 'You can sell a presidential candidate like you sell soap.' Once Nixon gave the word: 'We're going to build this whole campaign around television… you fellows just tell me what you want me to do and I'll do it.' the advertising men, public relations men, copywriters, makeup artist, photographers, and others joined together to create the image and the aura that would make this man America's favorite 'brand.'

These and other cases suggest that the art of selling cigarettes, soap, or steel may have some bearing on the art of selling social causes. People like McGinniss – and before him John K. Galbraith and Vance Packard – believe everything and anything can be sold by Madison Avenue, while people like Wiebe feel this is exaggerated. To the extent that Madison Avenue has this power, some persons would be heartened because of the many good causes in need of an effective social marketing technology, and others would despair over the spectre of mass manipulation.

Unfortunately there are few careful discussions of the power and limitations of social marketing. It is the authors' view that social marketing is a promising framework for planning and implementing social change. At the same time, it is poorly understood and often viewed suspiciously by many behavioral scientists. The application of commercial ideas and methods to promote social goals will be seen by many as another example of business's lack of taste and self-restraint. Yet the application of the logic of marketing to social goals is a natural development and on the whole a promising one. The idea will not disappear by ignoring it or ralling against it.

This article discusses the meaning, power, and limitations of social marketing as an approach to planned social change. First, this will require delineating the generic nature of marketing phenomena and some recent

Can marketing concepts and techniques be effectively applied to the promotion of social objectives such as brotherhood, safe driving, and family planning? The applicability of marketing concepts to such social problems is examined in this article. The authors show how social causes can be advanced more successfully through applying principles of marketing analysis, planning, and control to problems of social change.

conceptual developments in the marketing field. This will be followed by a definition of social marketing and an examination of the conditions under which it may be carried out effectively. The instruments of social marketing are defined, followed by a systems view of the application of marketing logic to social objectives.

What is Marketing?

The following statement testifies that there is no universal agreement on what marketing is.

> It has been described by one person or another as a business activity; as a group of related business activities; as a trade phenomenon; as a frame of mind; as a coordinative, integrative function in policy making; as a sense of business purpose; as an economic process; as a structure of institutions; as the process of exchanging or transferring ownership of products; as a process of concentration, equalization, and dispersion; as the creation of time, place and possession utilities; as a process of demand and supply adjustment; and many other things.[3]

> In spite of the confusing jumble of definitions, the core idea of marketing lies in *the exchange process. Marketing does not occur unless there are two or more parties, each with something to exchange, and both able to carry out communications and distribution.* Typically the subject of marketing is the exchange of goods or services for other goods or services or for money. Belshaw, in a excellent study of marketing exchange and its evolution from traditional to modern markets, shows the exchange process in marketing to be a fundamental aspect of both primitive and advanced social life.[4]

Given that the core idea of marketing lies in exchange processes, another concept can be postulated, that of marketing management, which can be defined as:

> Marketing management is the analysis, planning, implementation, and control of programs designed to bring about desired exchanges with target audiences for the purpose of personal or mutual gain. It relies heavily on the adaptation and coordination of product, price, promotion, and place for achieving effective response.[5]

> *Thus marketing management occurs when people become conscious of an opportunity to gain from a more careful planning of their exchange relations.* Although planned social change is not often viewed from the client's point of view, it involves very much an exchange relationship between client and change agent.

The practice of marketing management as applied to products and services has become increasingly sophisticated. The responsibility of launching new products on a national basis involving the investment and risk of millions of dollars and the uncertainties of consumer and competitor responses, has led to an increased reliance on formal research and planning throughout the product development and introduction cycle. Marketing management examines the wants, attitudes, and behavior of potential customers which could aid in designing a desired product and in merchandising, promoting, and distributing it successfully. Management goes through a formal process of strategy determination, tactical programming, regional and national implementation, performance measure, and feedback control.

There has been a shift from a sales to a marketing orientation in recent years. A sales orientation considers the job as one of finding customers for existing products and convincing them to buy these products. This sales concept is implicit in *The Selling of the President 1968*, since one is actually not developing a new 'product' for the job but rather trying to sell a given one with a suggestion that it is somewhat 'new and improved'. The marketing concept, on the other hand, calls for most of the effort to be spent on discovering the wants of a target audience and then creating the goods and services to satisfy them. This view seems privately and socially more acceptable. In private terms, the seller recognizes that it is easier to create products and services for existing wants than to try to alter wants and attitudes toward existing products. In social terms, it is held that this marketing philosophy restores consumer sovereignty in the determination of the society's product mix and the use of national resources.

In practice, since at any time there are both products in existence and new products being born, most marketing efforts are a mixture of selling and marketing; that is, a change strategy and a response strategy. In both cases, marketing management is becoming a sophisticated action technology that draws heavily on the behavioral sciences for clues to solving problems of communication and persuasion related to influencing the acceptability of commercial products and services. In the hands of its best practitioners, marketing management is applied behavioral science.

Social Marketing

An increasing number of nonbusiness institutions have begun to examine marketing logic as a means to furthering their institutional goals and products. Marketing men have advised churches on how to increase membership, charities on how to raise money, and art museums and symphonies on how to attract more patrons. In the social sphere, the Advertising Council of America has conducted campaigns for social objectives including 'Smokey the Bear,' 'Keep America Beautiful,' 'Joining the Peace Corps,' 'Buy Bonds,' and 'Go to College.' In fact, social advertising has become an established phenomenon on the American scene. Sandage says:

> True, (advertising's) communication function has been confined largely to informing and persuading people in respect to products and services. On the other hand, it can be made equally available to those who wish to inform and persuade people in respect to a city bond issue, cleaning up community crime, the 'logic' of atheism, the needs for better educational facilities, the abusive tactics of given law and enforcement

offices, or any other sentiment held by an individual who wishes to present such sentiment to the public.[7]

Social advertising has become such a feature of American society that it is no longer a question of whether to use it, but how to use it. It has been very successful in some cases and conspicuously unsuccessful in others. At fault to a large extent is the tendency of social campaigners to assign advertising the primary, if not the exclusive, role in accomplishing their social objectives. This ignores the marketing truism that a given marketing objective requires the coordination of the promotional mix with the goods and services mix and with the distribution mix. Social marketing is a much larger idea than social advertising and even social communication. To emphasize this, the authors define social marketing in the following way:

> Social marketing is the design, implementation, and control of programs calculated to influence the acceptability of social ideas and involving considerations of product planning, pricing, communication, distribution, and marketing research.

Thus, it is the explicit use of marketing skills to help translate present social action efforts into more effectively designed and communicated programs that elicit desired audience response. In other words, marketing techniques are the bridging mechanisms between the simple possession of knowledge and the socially useful implementation of what knowledge allows.

The Requisite Conditions for Effective Social Marketing

Lazarsfeld and Merton's Analysis

Lazarsfeld and Merton took exception with the view of many people that mass media can easily be used to control people's minds: 'It is our tentative judgment that the social role played by the very existence of the mass media has been commonly overestimated'.[9] Lazarsfeld and Merton, same reference as footnote 8, p. 462 They believed that the effectiveness of mass media for propaganda purposes depended on three conditions, one or more of which is lacking in most propaganda situations. The first condition is real or psychological *monopolization* by the media; that is, a condition marked by the absence of counterpropaganda. This characterizes the totalitarian state and accounts for the grater effectiveness of these regimes in molding public opinion through mass media. It is found occasionally in free societies under special circumstances, such as a wartime effort. For example, Kate Smith's effectiveness in selling war bonds over the radio during World Ward II was partially due to the marathon nature of the event and the fact that everyone believed in the cause: i.e., there was no counterpropaganda. However, most campaigns in a free society in peace time compete with so many other causes and everyday distractions that the monopoly condition is lacking, and this condition reduces the effectiveness of such campaigns.

Lazarsfeld and Merton said the second condition required for effective mass propaganda is *canalization*, the presence of an existing attitudinal base for the feelings that the social communications are striving to shape. They asserted that typical commercial advertising is effective because the task is not one of instilling basic new attitudes or creating significantly new behavior patterns, but rather canalizing existing attitudes and behavior in one direction or another. Thus, the seller of toothpaste does not have to socialize persons into new dental care habits, but rather into which brand of a familiar and desired product to purchase. If the pre-existing attitudes are present, then promotional campaigns are more effective, since canalization is always an easier task than social reconditioning.

The authors accept this idea but would add that many business marketing situations also involve the task of reshaping basic attitudes rather than canalizing existing ones. For example, consider business efforts to influence farmers to change time-honored farming practices, doctors to try out new drugs, and males to dress with more fashion and flair. Canalization is always easier, but the authors would like to emphasize that business marketers, like social marketers, often try to diffuse fundamentally new products and services which require major attitudinal reorientations.

Lazarsfeld and Merton call the third condition *supplementation* by which they mean the effort to follow up mass communication campaigns with programs of face-to-face contacts. In trying to explain the success of the rightist Father Coughlin movement in the thirties. Lazarsfeld and Merton observe:

> This combination of a central supply propaganda (Coughlin's addresses on a nationwide network), the coordinated distribution of newspapers and pamphlets and locally organized face-to-face discussions among relatively small groups – this complex of reciprocal reinforcement by mass media and personal relations proved spectacularly successful.[10]

This approach is standard in many closed societies and organizations and suggests another key difference between social advertising and social marketing. Whereas a social advertising approach contrives only the event of mass media communication and leaves the response to natural social processes, social marketing arranges for a stepdown communication process. The message is passed on and discussed in more familiar surroundings to increase its memorability, penetration, and action consequences. Thus supplementation, monopolization, and canalization are critical factors influencing the effectiveness of any social marketing effort.

Wiebe's Analysis

An additional contribution was made by Wiebe in his attempt to understand the differential effectiveness of four social campaigns.[11] He explained the relative effectiveness of these campaigns in terms of the audience member's experience with regard to five factors:

1 *The Force.* The intensity of the person's motivation toward the goal as a combination of his predisposition prior to the message and the stimulation of the message.

2 *The Direction.* Knowledge of how or where the person might go to consummate his motivation.

3 *The Mechanism.* The existence of an agency that enables the person to translate his motivation into action.

4 *Adequacy and Compatibility.* The ability and effectiveness of the agency in performing its task.

5 *Distance.* The audience member's estimate of the energy and cost required to consummate the motivation in relation to the reward.

To show how these factors operate, Wiebe first analyzed the Kate Smith campaign to sell bonds during World War II. This campaign was imminently successful, according to Wiebe, because of the presence of force (patriotism), direction (buy bonds), mechanism (banks, post offices, telephone orders), adequacy and compatibility (so many centers to purchase the bonds), and distance (ease of purchase). In fact, extra telephone lines were installed on the night of the campaign at 134 CBS stations to take orders during her appeal. The effort to buy bonds

> …was literally reduced to the distance between the listener and his telephone. Psychological distance was also minimized. The listener remained in his own home. There were no new people to meet, no unfamiliar procedures, no forms to fill out, no explanation, no waiting.[12]

In the case of a campaign to recruit Civil Defense volunteers, many of the same factors were present except that the social mechanism was not prepared to handle the large volume of response, and this reduced the campaign's success. Teachers, manuals, equipment, and registration and administration procedures were *inadequate*, and many responding citizens were turned away and disappointed after they were led to believe that their services were urgently needed.

The third campaign, a documentary on juvenile delinquency, did not meet with maximum success because of the *absence of a mechanism*. Instead of being directed to an existing agency, people were urged to form neighborhood councils themselves. This certainly takes far more effort than simply picking up the phone to buy a war bond, or 'stopping in' to register at the nearest Civil Defense unit.

The fourth campaign revolved around the goal of the Kefauver committee hearings to arouse citizens to 'set their house in order.' This campaign met with a notable lack of success, however, because citizens were not *directed* to an appropriate mechanism despite the fact that one existed in principle in the political party organizations. Political party organizations apparently left much to be desired in terms of availability and compatibility. The skepticism prevalent at the time concerning the chances of anything beneficial happening as a result of the hearings was ample evidence that considerable psychological distance existed between the audience and the mechanisms for action.

The Social Marketing Approach

The Lazarsfeld and Merton conditions and the Wiebe factors provide a useful background for viewing the conceptual framework used by marketing strategists. Marketers view the marketing problem as one of developing the right *product* backed by the right *promotion* and put in the right *place* at the right *price*. These key variables in the marketing mix have been named the four P's by McCarthy.[13] The authors shall examine each of these variables, in terms of some well-known social issues.

Product. In business marketing, sellers study the needs and wants of target buyers and attempt to design products and services that meet their desires. If well-designed and affordable, these products will be purchased. In social marketing, sellers also have to study the target audiences and design appropriate products. They must 'package' the social idea in a manner which their target audiences find desirable and are willing to purchase. This corresponds to Wiebe's idea of a mechanism.

Product design is typically more challenging in the social area than it is in the business area. Consider the problem of marketing 'safer driving.' The social objective is to create safer driving habits and attitudes in the population. There is no one product that can accomplish this. Various products have to be designed that will make partial contributions to the social objective. A public education media campaign providing tips on safe driving is one such product; the offering of 'defensive driving courses' is another; the creation of insurance policies which reduce premiums for safer drivers is still another product. In general, the social marketer remains aware of the *core product* (safer driving) and tries to create various tangible products and services which are 'buyable' and which advance the social objective.

Identical reasoning is required by those who market *altruistic causes* (e.g., charity giving, blood donation), *personal health causes* (e.g., non-smoking, better nutrition), and *social betterment causes* (e.g., civil rights, improved housing, better environment). In each case, the social marketer must define the change sought, which may be a change in values, beliefs, affects, behavior, or some mixture. He must meaningfully segment the target markets. He must design social products for each market which are 'buyable,' and which instrumentally serve the social cause. In some social causes, the most difficult problem will be to innovate appropriate products; in other cases it will be to motivate purchase.

Promotion. The marketing man's second control variable is promotion. It is the communication persuasion strategy and tactics that will make the product familiar, acceptable, and even desirable to the audience. Wiebe's counterpart to promotion is 'force.' The social campaign strategist will tend to think of this as mass media communication, but promotion is actually a much larger idea. To the marketing man, promotion includes the following major activities:

Advertising: Any paid form of nonpersonal presentation and promotion of products, services, or ideas by an identified sponsor.

Personal Selling: Any paid form of personal presentation and promotion of products, service, or ideas by an identified sponsor.

Publicity: Any unpaid form of nonpersonal presentation and promotion of products, services, or ideas where the sponsor is unidentified.

Sales Promotion: Miscellaneous paid forms (special programs, incentives, materials, and events) designed to stimulate audience interest and acceptance of a product.

Each of these promotional tools involves complex issues in strategy and tactics. With respect to advertising, the marketer has to determine the size of the total advertising budget, the choice of appeals, the development of attention-getting copy, the selection of effective and efficient media, the scheduling of the advertising inputs, and the measurement of overall and segment-level results. With respect to personal selling, the marketer must determine the size of the total sales force, the development of sales territory boundaries and assignments, the development of personal presentation strategies, the degree and type of salesforce motivation and supervision, and the evaluation of salesforce effectiveness. Publicity necessitates arranging for significant news about the product to appear in various media. Sales promotion calls for developing special display, premiums, programs, and events that might be useful in stimulating interest or action.

Each of these activities is a specialty in which the experts have achieved sophisticated levels of knowledge and techniques. This is especially apparent when one examines social campaigns developed by amateurs where the appeals and copy seem very naïve. Even behavioral science consultants to social campaign organizations often fail to make a maximum contribution because of their inability or reluctance to view the issue in broad marketing terms instead of in strictly social or ethical terms.

Recently Nathaniel Martin criticized the Indian government for failing to handle family planning as a marketing problem.

> Selling birth control is as much a marketing job as selling any other consumer product. And where no manufacturer would contemplate developing and introducing a new product without a thorough understanding of the variables of the market, planners in the highest circles of Indian government have blithely gone ahead without understanding that marketing principles must determine the character of any campaign of voluntary control. The Indians have done only the poorest research. They have mismanaged distribution of contraceptive devices. They have ignored the important of 'customer service.' They have proceeded with grossly inadequate undertrained staffs; they have been blind to the importance of promotion and advertising.[14]

> This is not to deny that the Indian government has undertaken some innovative promotional approaches. Referral fees are paid to salesmen, barbers, and others who bring in consenting males for sterilization. The consenting male is given a transistor radio or a small payment to cover his costs of being absent from work. Women have been offered gifts for consenting to use intrauterine contraceptive devices. But Martin feels that the total program lacks the qualities of an organized, well planned, and continuous marketing effort. [15]

An example of careful promotional planning for a social objective is found in the American Cancer Society efforts to raise money for cancer research. In their brochure directed to local units, they attempt to educate the volunteer and professional chapters on the handling of newspapers, pictures, company publication, radio and television, movies, special events, and controversial arguments. For example, in terms of special events:

> Dramatic special events attract attention to the American Cancer Society. They bring color, excitement, and glamour to the program. Well planned, they will get excellent coverage in newspapers, on radio and TV, and in newsreels.

> A Lights-on-Drive, a one-afternoon or one-night House-to-House program have such dramatic appeal that they stir excitement and enthusiasm... keep in mind the value of bursts of sound such as fire sirens sounding, loud-speaker trucks, fife and drum corps... A most useful special event is the ringing of church bells to add a solemn, dedicated note to the launching of a drive or education project. This should be organized on a Division or community basis, and the church bell ringing may be the signal to begin a House-to-House canvass. Rehearsals of bell ringing, community leaders tugging at ropes, offer good picture possibilities.[16]

Some readers might be critical of this approach to a worthwhile social objective, but two things should be mentioned. The first is that this should not be identified as the *marketing approach to social objectives*. Many persons mistakenly assume that marketing means hard selling. This is only a particular style of marketing, and it has its critics both inside and outside the profession. There are many firms that market their products with taste and sensitivity; examples include Xerox, Container Corporation, and Hallmark. It is important to recognize that this is not nonmarketing but rather a style of marketing that was chosen in the belief of its greater effectiveness in accomplishing the goals of the organization.

Second, the issue is not whether a particular approach suits one's personal taste, but whether it works. If a 'hard' marketing style raises substantially more money for cancer research than a 'soft' marketing style, it must be respected by those who think cancer research is more important than personal aesthetics.

Place. The third element of the marketing approach to social campaigns calls for providing adequate and compatible distribution and response channels. Motivated persons should know where the product can be obtained. Place is equivalent to two of Wiebe's five conditions for an effective mass communication campaign (direction, and adequacy and compatibility). The poor results of many social campaigns can be attributed in part to their failure to suggest clear action outlets for those motivated to acquire the product. The current campaign to interest people in the pollution problem may suffer from this defect. It is succeeding in making everyone not only aware of environmental pollution but also fearful of it. People want to do something about it. But for the most part they cannot act because there is not a clear product to 'buy' (such as a petition to sign, an election in which to choose an antipollution candidate, or a pending piece of national legislation). Nor does the average person have a clear picture of the alternative channels of action for expressing his interest in the issue. There are so many ad hoc organizations working without coordination and at times with cross-purpose, that the average person is likely to 'tune out' from further messages because of personal frustration. Saturation campaigns unaccompanied by the provision of adequate response channels may result in 'interest overkill.'

The importance of place has been recognized in several campaigns. The most notable example is the Kate Smith bond-selling campaign and its imaginative establishment of telephone order channels during the broadcast. Strategists of anticigarette campaigns have recognized the need for action channels by setting up smoker's clinics in many large cities. They could even go further and provide telephone advice and even social calls if the economics would justify these additional channels. An advertising agency is planning a campaign called 'Pick Your Issue' in which several different social issues would be individually featured. The point would be made that because the busy citizen does not have time to become involved in all issues, this should not be an excuse to remain uninvolved in any issues. The good citizen should 'pick an issue.' Each issue advertisement will contain information on the organizations active in that area and inform the citizen about where to write for further information.

Thus, place means arranging for accessible outlets which permit the translation of motivations into actions. Planning in this area entails selecting or developing appropriate outlets, deciding on their number, average size, and locations, and giving them proper motivation to perform their part of the job.

Price. The final control variable that must be planned is price. Price represents the costs that the buyer must accept in order to obtain the product. It resembles Wiebe's concept of distance and incorporates some aspects of adequacy and compatibility. Price includes money cost, opportunity cost, energy costs, and psychic costs. Thus, the cost to persons asked to appear for immunization shots includes any possible money charge, any opportunities foregone, the expenditure of energy, and the psychological concerns aroused by inoculation.

The cost of giving up smoking is largely psychological, since there is actually a financial saving in breaking the habit. The cost of using seat belts is the charge for buying them, the effort to lock and unlock them, and the psychological cost of not being completely sure one is better off in an accident wearing them or not wearing them.

The functioning of this concept can also be illustrated in terms of an interesting phenomenon in health care services where many poor patients prefer to patronize unlicensed practitioners and pay a fee instead of going to the free hospital. In Caracas, Venezuela, for example, although there is a free hospital for the indigent, many of them patronize private clinics which cost them 20 bolivares for consultation. Why? Because while there is no charge at the free hospital, there is substantial cost to the patient in terms of energy and psychological abuse. When a patient arrives at the hospital, he has to wait to see a social worker first. When he is finally interviewed, the social worker asks many questions about his income to determine whether he is really indigent. Then he sees a number of other hospital staff members for various tests, and again is asked about his income. Finally, he sees the doctor who might discover that he really needs to see a specialist who will not be available for several weeks. Throughout the experience, the person is made to feel inferior and a nuisance. Therefore, it is not surprising that he wishes to avoid these energy and psychological costs even if it means paying for the services.

But even monetary charges may play a useful role in leading the poor back to free hospital services. In private correspondence, a social psychologist suggested:

> It is a surprising discovery that even free medical care presents a marketing problem. Maybe we should apply dissonance theory and introduce such medical care at a high price to make it look more desirable. Then let us apply a cents-off special introductory offer to make the service attractive.

The marketing man's approach to pricing the social product is based on the assumption that members of a target audience perform a cost-benefit analysis when considering the investment of money, time, or energy in the issue. They somehow process the major benefits and compare them to the major costs, and the strength of their motivation to act is directly related to the magnitude of the excess benefit. This type of conceptualization of behavior is found not only in the economist's model of economic man, but also in behavioristic theory with its emphasis on rewards and costs, in Gestalt theory with its emphasis on positive and negative valences, and in management theory with its emphasis on incentives and constraints. The marketer's approach to selling a social product is to consider how the rewards for buying the product can be increased relative to the costs, or the costs reduced relative to the rewards, or trying to find a mix of product, promotion, place, and price that will simultaneously increase the rewards and reduce the costs. The main point is that social marketing requires that careful thought be given to the manner in which manageable, desirable, gratifying, and convenient solutions to a perceived need or problem are presented to its potential buyers.

The Social Marketing Planning Process

The 'four P's' of marketing management are integrated in an administrative process framework in Figure 1. Continuous information is collected from the *environment* by the *change agency. Plans and messages* are created and sent through *channels to audiences,* and the results are monitored by the *change agency.*

The change agency operates a research unit and a planning unit. The research unit collects several types of information. It monitors the environment – economic, political, technological, cultural, and competitive influences – for important developments affecting its social policies and objectives. For example, a family planning agency would monitor economic-

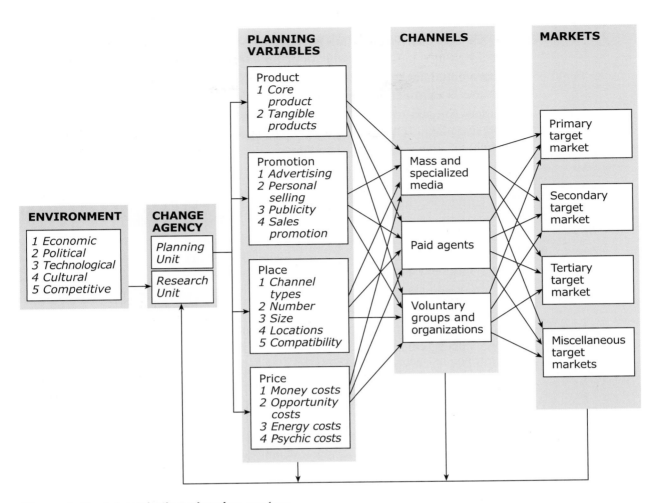

Figure 1: Social marketing planning system

demographic developments (income and population trends), political developments (liberalization of birth control information), technological developments (new birth control techniques and devices), cultural developments (attitudinal changes toward birth control), and competitive developments (actions of similar and competing groups). The research unit also collects information on the past effectiveness of various programs as well as information on audience attitudes, desires, and behavior.

The change agent's planning unit formulates short- and long-range social marketing plans on the basis of this information. For example, the family planning organization carefully considers the role of different products, promotions, places, and prices. It would identify the major channels of communication and distribution, such as mass or specialized media, paid agents, and volunteer groups. It would differentiate the programs intended for its primary target market (large and low-income families), secondary target market (other childbearing families), tertiary target market (sources of funds and additional volunteer efforts), and miscellaneous target markets (politicians and church groups). Finally, it would continuously gather effectiveness measures on these programs for recycling its planning.

This approach represents an application of business marketing principles to the problem of marketing social change. It is already manifest in some of the larger social change agencies. For example, consider the work of the National Safety Council. Its staff includes an advertising manager, a sales promotion management, Advertising Council of America coordinator, a research director, and a program director. One of its products is a defensive driving course. Figure 2 shows the various channels through which this course is marketed along with the promotional tools it uses. The National Safety Council reaches potential prospects through business firms, service organizations, schools, and the police and court system. For the 1970s, the National Safety Council has adopted

> ... a four point marketing program. ... One of the first objectives is to increase the sales effectiveness of our existing 150 state and local safety council cooperating agencies. ... The second part of the program is to create 500 new training agencies in communities not now served by safety councils. ... A third part of the marketing program will be aimed at selling big industry on adopting DDC as a training course for all employees or selected categories of employees in plant-run training programs. ... The fourth part of the marketing plan deals with a nationwide promotional effort built around a series of community special-emphasis campaigns running from February 1 through Memorial Day each year of the decade.[17]

This example illustrates the possibilities of the marketing approach for furthering social causes. The National Safety Council and several other social agencies have graduated from occasional campaign organizations to full-time marketing organizations which go through cycles of information gathering, planning, product development, measuring, and reprogramming.

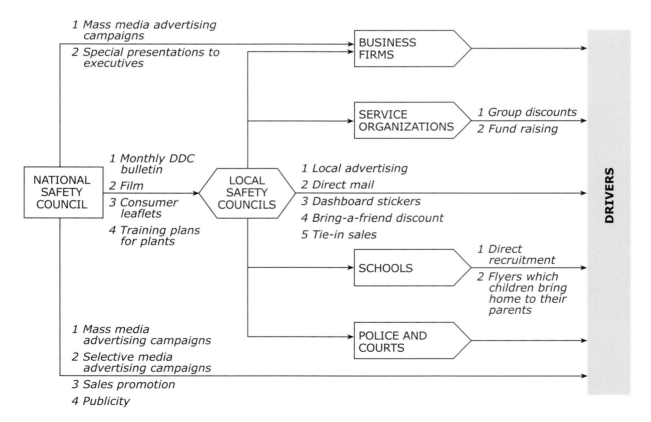

Figure 2: Marketing channels and tools: Defensive driving course

Social Implications of Social Marketing

The authors believe that specific social causes could benefit from marketing thinking and planning. Problems of pollution control, mass transit, private education, drug abuse, and public medicine are in need of innovative solutions and approaches for gaining public attention and support. Marketing men by their training are finely attuned to market needs, product development, pricing and channel issues, and mass communication and promotion techniques, all of which are critical in the social area.

At the same time, social marketing is sufficiently distinct from business marketing to require fresh thinking and new approaches. Social marketing typically has to deal with the market's core beliefs and values, whereas business marketing often deals with superficial preferences and opinions. Social marketing must search harder for meaningful *quid pro quos* to gain acceptance or adoption of its products. Social marketing has to work with channel systems that are less well-defined and less pecuniarily motivated. Only through applying marketing concepts and tools to a large number of cases will the powers and limits of the social marketing approach be learned.

In addition, there is the definite possibility that the overt marketing of social objectives will be resented and resisted. There will be charges that it is 'manipulative,' and consequently contributes to bringing the society closer to Orwell's 1984. There will be charges that even if not manipulative, social marketing will increase the amount of 'promotional noise' in the society, which is found distasteful both because it emphasizes 'trivial differences' and because it is 'noise.' Finally, social marketing will be accused of increasing the costs of promoting social causes beyond the point of a net gain either to the specific cause or the society as a whole. In the charities industry, professional marketing increases the absolute cost of raising money, but it usually succeeds in raising more money after these costs are taken into account. However, when one considers the entire picture, it is possible that the total amount donated to charities may not increase by the same amount as the professional marketing costs.

The authors are concerned with these possible dysfunctional consequences, and they must obviously be subtracted from the potential benefits that social marketing might produce. Since social marketing is just emerging, those concerned are encouraged to monitor it closely in the same dispassionate spirit that business marketers have so ably analyzed and documented the many manifestations of business marketing practice over the years.

Summary

This article considered the applicability of marketing concepts to the problem of promoting social causes. Social marketing was defined as the design, implementation, and control of programs calculated to influence the acceptability of social ideas and involving considerations of product planning, pricing, communication, distribution, and marketing research.

Too often, social advertising rather than social marketing is practiced by social campaigners. Lazarsfeld and Merton attributed the failure of many social advertising campaigns to the frequent absence of conditions of monopolization, canalization, and supplementation in the social arena. Wiebe, in his examination of four campaigns, concluded that a campaign's effectiveness depended on the presence of adequate force, direction, and adequate and compatible social mechanism, and distance. To the marketer, the success of the campaign depends on the proper development of product, promotion, place, and price considerations. These concepts were defined and were shown to have applicability to social causes. The social marketing process calls for marketing research and the subsequent development of a well-conceived product and appeals moving through mass and specialized communication media and through paid agents and voluntary groups to reach targeted audiences. The marketing style may be hard or soft, depending on which is deemed most effective in accomplishing the social objectives.

A marketing planning approach does not guarantee that the social objectives will be achieved, or that the costs will be acceptable. Yet social marketing appears to represent a bridging mechanism which links the behavioral scientist's knowledge of human behavior with the socially useful implementation of what that knowledge allows. It offers a useful framework for effective social planning at a time when social issues have become more relevant and critical.

MARKETING MEMO

The Marketing Concept and Technology...

... It is a mistake to think of technology as entirely autonomous, although it has secured for itself a great deal of autonomy. And it is a mistake to think that the technological system is self-justifying in its own terms. The present ecological crisis and fundamental rethinking of technology's role in the society of the future is the *prima facie* illustration of this point. We are going to abandon many technological developments even though the existing technological order justifies their further development. We are going to introduce many new technologies for which there is no need in the existing technological system. And we are going to evolve and invent many new forms of technological knowledge which are either unnecessary or simply go against the grain of the existing technological system. We are going to do these things because we are in process of changing the nature of the dialogue concerning the needs of society and the potentials of technology.

> — Henryk Skolimowski, "Problems of Truth in Technology," *Ingenor 8* (Winter, 1970/71, College of Engineering, The University of Michigan), pp. 5-7, 41-46, at p. 42.

ABOUT THE AUTHORS. Philip Kotler is A. Montgomery Ward Professor of Marketing at the Graduate School of Management, Northwestern

University. He is the author of *Marketing Management: Analysis, Planning and Control* and *Marketing Decision Making; A Model-Building Approach.* Professor Kotler is also advisory editor of the Holt, Rinehart and Winston Marketing Series, former chairman of the College on Marketing of the Institute of Management Sciences, and presently a director of the American Marketing Association.

Gerald Zaltman is associate professor of behavioral science. Department of Marketing, Graduate School of Management and Faculty Associate of the Center for the Interdisciplinary Study of Science and Technology at Northwestern University. He holds an MBA degree from The University of Chicago and a PhD in sociology from The Johns Hopkins University. Professor Zaltman is author of *Marketing: Contributions from the Behavioral Sciences, co-editor of Creating Social Change* (in press), *Perspectives on Social Change* (in press), and a contributor to numerous books and journals. His major research interests and writing concern the diffusion of innovations, communication, social change, and the sociology of science.

The authors would like to express their appreciation to the Educational Foundation of the American Association of Advertising Agencies for their support which permitted activities leading to many of the ideas expressed in this article.

[1] G. D. Wiebe, 'Merchandising Commodities and Citizenship on Television,' *Public Opinion Quarterly*, Vol. 15 (Winter, 1951-52), pp. 679-691, at p. 679.

[2] Joe McGiniss, *The Selling of the President 1968* (New York: Trident Press, 1969).

[3] Marketing Staff of the Ohio State University, 'A Statement of Marketing Philosophy,' JOURNAL OF MARKETING, Vol. 29 (January, 1965), p. 43.

[4] Cyril S. Belshaw, *Traditional Exchange and Modern Markets* (Englewood Cliffs, N.J.: Prentice-Hall, Inc., 1965).

[5] Philip Kotler, *Marketing Management: Analysis, Planning and Control*, Second Editions (Englewood Cliffs, N.J.: Prentice-Hall, Inc., 1972).

[6] Arthur H. Niehoff, *A Casebook of Social Change* (Chicago: Aldine, 1966); Warren G. Bennis, Kenneth D. Benne and Robert Chin, *The Planning of Change* (New York: Holt, Rinehart & Winston, 1969).

[7] C. H. Sandage, 'Using Advertising to Implement the Concept of Freedom of Speech,' in *The Role of Advertising*, .C. H. Sandage and V. Fryburger, eds. (Homewood, Ill.: Richard D. Irwin, Inc., 1960), pp. 222-223.

[8] Paul F. Lazarsfeld and Robert K. Merton, 'Mass Communications, Popular Taste, and Organized Social Action,' in *Mass Communications*, William Schramm, ed. (Urbana, Ill.: University of Illinois Press, 1949), pp. 459-480, and the same reference as footnote 1.

[9] Lazarsfeld and Merton, same reference as footnote 8, p462.

[10] Lazarsfeld and Merton, same reference as footnote 8.

[11] Same reference as footnote 1.

[12] Same reference as footnote 1, p. 633.

[13] E. Jerome McCarthy, *Basic Marketing: A Managerial Approach*, Third Edition, (Homewood, III.: Richard D. Irwin, Inc., 1968), pp. 31–33.

[14] Nathaniel A. Martin, 'The Outlandish Idea: How a Marketing Man Would Save India,' *Marketing/Communications*, Vol. 297 (March 1968), pp. 54-60.

[15] For two analyses of the marketing issues and opportunities in the family planning issue, see Julian L. Simon, 'A Huge Marketing Research Task – Birth Control,' *Journal of Marketing Research*, Vol. 5 (February, 1968), pp. 21-27; and Glen L. Urban, 'Ideas on a Decision-Information System for Family Planning,' *Industrial Management Review*, Vol. 10 (Spring, 1969), pp. 45-61.

[16] *Public Information Guide* (New York: American Cancer Society, Inc., 1965), p. 19.

[17] Chris Imhoff, 'DDC'S Decisive Decade,' *Traffic Safety Magazine*, Vol. 69 (December 1969), pp. 20 and 36.

Module team

B324 module team

Fiona Harris (*Co-Module Team Chair*)
Anne Smith (*Co-Module Team Chair*)
Mike Green (*Author*)
David Faulkner (*Consultant, Responsible Business Marketing*)
June Payne/Wayne Oakes (*Module Manager*)
Kelly Dobbs (*Module Team Assistant*)
Steve Godrich (*Regional Manager*)
Gerard Hastings (*Consultant*)
Mike Lucas (*Undergraduate Programme Director*)
Alan Tapp, Professor and Research Unit Director, Bristol Business School
(*External Assessor*)

Module production

Holly Clements (*Rights and Picture Research*)
Jonathan Davies (*Graphic Designer*)
Hannah Eiseman-Renyard (*Editor)*
Julie Fletcher (*Media Project Manager*)
Edwina Jones (*Editor)*
Grant Miller (*Conferencing*)
Dave Richings (*Print Buying Coordinator*)
Kelvin Street (*Library*)